D1557742

OLIVER CROMWELL
Pretender, Puritan, Statesman, Paradox ?

Edited by JOHN F. H. NEW
University of Waterloo

HOLT, RINEHART AND WINSTON
New York • Chicago • San Francisco • Atlanta
Dallas • Montreal • Toronto • London • Sydney

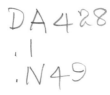
Cover Illustration: Oliver Cromwell. Anonomous engraving. 19th Century. *(New York Public Library)*

CONTENTS

INTRODUCTION

Biography is probably the oldest and certainly the most popular form of history. It is a form that has never shed its links with mythology and imaginative literature, which poses special problems for the student of history who expects interpretation to be congruent with the evidence and approximate to the truth. Forceful figures are inclined to attract or repel those who examine their doings minutely, and Cromwell has had his ardent worshipers and his revilers, both contemporary and modern. That his admirers and denigrators can be found in Conservative, Whig, liberal, or radical camps is evidence of the difficulty of any biographical form's capturing reality, a difficulty compounded with a subject as elusive as Cromwell.

Few contemporaries boasted that they really knew Cromwell. Perhaps he did not know himself. He thought of himself as an ordinary Englishman, yet it is apparent that he was an extraordinary man. Cromwell rose to greatness suddenly, and in middle age; but unlike others whose rise was swift, he was never an adventurer in politics, nor a wayward genius whose life's blood was refreshed by political play. Despite the charges of the jealous and the alienated, he seems to have had no lust for high office and no pretensions to pomp and circumstance.

One tends to think of Cromwell as the spawn of the revolution, thrown to prominence and power in the cataract of events after 1642, and to forget that he was also a cause of the revolution, embodying in his person some of the sources of discontent in the kingdom and nurturing the bracing spirit which made the waging of a civil war both thinkable and feasible.

Cromwell was a plain country squire, not an aristocrat, and that is instructive. After the failure of England in the Hundred Years War and the desperate internecine squabbles, known as the War of the Roses, which followed, the feudal nobility declined as a source of power and a seat of counterauthority to the Crown. The pacification of the nobility, a watershed in Western history, occurred fairly early in England. Crowned heads had less to fear from their overmighty barony than from their less vaunted but more populous gentry and middle classes.

Cromwell was of the middling sort of gentry, neither rising dramatically nor declining inexorably. Raised with a sense of command, by virtue of his being raised a gentleman, his middling position allowed him a broader range of social contact than he might otherwise have enjoyed. He could speak as easily to lords

1

as to artisans in a manner that was impossible for those of higher or lower condition. As a gentleman who had been educated at Cambridge and the Inns of Court, he was not atypical of the leading contenders on both sides of the Civil War. It was a war between sections of the influential sectors of society, essentially, with more nobility cleaving to the Crown as the source of honor, and more urban artisans and petitbourgeois risking their blood for Parliament. In terms of leadership, however, one must not overdraw social distinctions.

Cromwell was middle-aged at the outbreak of civil war, and this is also revealing. He was typical of the Parliamentary party as a whole, for detailed studies of the membership of the Long Parliament show, curiously enough, that they were, on the average, a decade older than the loyalists. The rebellion was not the rebellion of the young but of older stagers whose grievances against the Crown were begun in James's reign and case-hardened under Charles. Clarendon's verdict that the story of the revolution need not begin before 1625 cannot be accepted for it would appear that the seed time was in the first and second decades of the century.

After the rapid growth of Commons' self-consciousness early in James's reign, it is sometimes forgotten that, the Addled Parliament aside, James ruled without Parliament for as long a span as his son. In the subsequent period, under the rule of the Duke of Buckingham, the eagerness of the Commons to retain and even enlarge their privileges in the face of assumed prerogative encroachments blossomed into a constitutional revolution. The Petition of Right may be said to amount to an intended constitutional revolution in which the liberty and property of the subject was to be protected against the Crown, especially against the Crown's increasing influence over the judiciary. By the Petition, the House of Commons would have been moved into a position to play an indispensable role in the government of the realm.

In fact, the Petition, which Cromwell warmly supported, became a moribund monument of intention as soon as it was given the royal assent in statutory form. Charles made it clear that he was intransigently opposed to its spirit and its substance.

From the Petitioners' point of view the eleven years of personal rule that followed were a subversion of agreed constitutional arrangements. The government's desperate financial expedients—the knighthood fines, the penalties for infringing old forest laws, ship money, the continued levies on tonnage and poundage—destroyed the essence of all that the Parliamentarians of the 1620's had fought for. What followed the Parliament of 1628–1629 appeared to them a counter-revolution. The government's policies, upheld by legal decisions, and designed to salvage the Crown from insolvency, to guarantee the national safety, and to coerce malcontents in the interests of good order and government were read by the opposition as dangerous infringements on the life and liberty of the subjects and as threats to the security of property. This radical separation of perceptions was to stain all political negotiations thereafter and to sour the atmosphere throughout the civil wars to the final trial and execution of the King.

The Puritan opposition to the Crown can also be traced to the first and second decades of the century or, even earlier, to ecclesiastical disputes under Elizabeth. Here again, Cromwell's age is a significant pointer, for at the beginning of the reign of James I, the close and rigid policies of Archbishop Bancroft ended all hope of containing the majority of English Puritans peaceably within the church.

Puritan demands had been met with initial harshness under James, so more Puritans began to separate from the Establishment, setting up voluntary congregations. More important was the majority of those called Puritans who separated themselves spiritually if not actually from the Church of England by adopting a markedly higher standard of moral rectitude than was customary in the church. Moral rigorism and a mounting clamor of censoriousness toward the lax court edged Puritanism into an alien and unsympathetic frame of mind. Against this frame, James's later dalliance with the Catholics; a Catholic match for Charles; bungled and dubious foreign ventures when international affairs were viewed in Manichaean fashion as struggles of Protestant light against Catholic darkness; and the emergence, near the crown, of a small group of high Anglicans who sought liturgical improvements smacking of Popery to the Puritans; all tend to enmesh political and religious opposition more closely together than ever before.

In such an atmosphere of misunderstanding, fear, and distrust, religious feelings played a decisive, if indirect, role. For, like most of his colleagues on the Parliamentary side, Cromwell was a Puritan. In fact, he was a more radical Puritan than most; at the same time, he was less strict about ecclesiastical forms and less sectarian in spirit than most.

While the House of Commons was claiming redress of constitutional grievances in the Parliaments between 1621 and 1628–1629, the Puritans were infiltrating the pulpits and parishes of the Establishment. Although they suffered setbacks—in 1633 Archbishop Laud was able to confiscate monies raised by the Puritans expressly for this purpose—their hold on the pulpits continued to be strong. By means of "lectureships" or "preacherships" independent of the curacies, vicarages, and rectories in the church, they managed to sprinkle London and other corporations with propagandists.

Laud's distaste for the lecturer and the Puritans' dislike of his liturgical improvements for "the beauty of holiness" established a chasm of distrust between Anglican and Puritan that parallels the distrust arising from the divergent glosses on the Petition of Right in the political sphere. The changes in emphasis and style which Laud pressed upon the Establishment were bitterly resented as treacherous and Popish by the Puritan Protestants. They saw in his insidious changes the harbingers of counter-Reformation. Laud, for his part, found Puritans' fear ill-grounded and incredible, and their activities subversive.

Cromwell once said of the Civil War that religion was not the thing at first contended for, but that God had brought it to that issue at last. He was thinking of the English scene only and placing prior weight on the struggle of the Commons to secure itself a permanent share in the executive arm of the English monarchy. Had he been thinking in larger terms, with Scotland in mind in particular, he might have made religion the first or prior occasion. For it was Laud's high-handed policy of imposing an Anglican uniformity on the Presbyterian Scots that caused an invasion of England and the straining of royal resources which forced, in turn, the calling of the Short and the Long Parliaments. The English Revolution flourished under the kilts of the Scots.

Few Puritans were rigid Scottish-style Presbyterians, but the bonds of religious sympathy laid the basis for later military collusion. It is significant that in the last resort almost all the Parliamentarians from the Long Parliament were Puritan and all but one or two of the Royalists were Anglican or Catholic. Religion had become an aspect of a more total array of social and political leanings. In the maze of alarms and doubts, religion was an index of just how far into opposition and how far toward the possible consequences of anarchy one would carry one's distrust. The deeper the fear, the further Parliamentarians felt they had to travel in setting up constitutional guarantees against "arbitrary" government.

Cromwell's military service was related to his Puritanism. His sense of discipline stemmed from the iron self-discipline he practiced as a Puritan. His peculiarly nonsectarian brand of ultra-Protestantism served him in recruiting as well. Indeed, as deliberate policy he recruited radical Puritans because he knew they would have the ideological stiffening that others might lack. His capacity to rationalize army organization cannot be traced to his Puritanism particularly, but the fervor of his military campaigns had distinctly religious overtones. Cromwell came to feel that his troops, and then his officers, were something like a gathered church—an interesting conjecture. Because his cavalry was never beaten, he came to think of it as a finger of Providence.

This sort of belief, which is so hard to disentangle from self-deception or even cynical rationalizing, led many contemporaries to view Cromwell as a dissembling hypocrite. James Heath's biography was influential in fixing the image of Cromwell in the public eye as a designing, ambitious schemer. Written after the Revolution, it reflects the popular orthodoxy of that period when vituperation had come into fashion, and when the nation wished to forget its immediate past by believing that Cromwell had imposed himself by main force and Machiavellianism upon an unwilling nation. Heath's biography laces fact with fancy—indeed, with scurrilous calumny. We have included a snippet of it partly to display the mixture of fable and truth that still passed for popular history at the time. The view that it expresses, however, is shared by some modern historians and came to be shared by some of Cromwell's old associates, who were not only anti-Royalists but outright republicans.

Ludlow's *Memoirs* also were written after the Restoration, from exile. They vindicate Ludlow as the true opponent of royalism. His consistent republicanism eventually led him to break with Cromwell, after he turned out the Rump of the Long Parliament in 1653, and to repudiate him altogether when he accepted the Protectorship of England in 1654. As Ludlow's *Memoirs* suggest—harking back to Hugh Peter who was chaplain to the Council of State—other associates had suspicions of Cromwell's plans before he became Lord Protector. Whereas Heath had never known Cromwell, Ludlow had been a personal friend; and the charges and distrust of former friends and comrades-in-arms wounded Cromwell deeply.

Since the republicans' fears of him were widespread and influential, Cromwell made answer in public, an answer that shows something of the self-analysis he undertook and the anguish he suffered as a result of their attitude. He appealed to them, not on political grounds, nor on the grounds of their having shared common dangers, but on the basis of their bonds of Puritanism. Events which were clearly the handiwork of God had led him, nay, forced him to assume the Protectorship. What was at issue between Cromwell and his royalist and republican opponents was his integrity. Indeed, it is a basic question for the student of history to consider on what evidence and what kind of evidence questions of such importance and such intimacy can be solved.

After years of work on Cromwell, Robert S. Paul concluded that Cromwell's religiosity had to be taken at face value. He saw Cromwell as a man caught in the perennial tensions between faith and political action. Cromwell was bound to search his soul and feel his way, because, like all Christians, he had to reconcile his understanding of God's plan for man with the trappings of earthly historical events. Like all Christians, too, he had to compromise continuously between the divine ethic of love and the earthly ethic of justice. Paul clearly believed that these sorts of adjustments are a part of the predicament of all active Christians. Thus, Cromwell's behavior is relevant to the modern situation: his broad conception of the church and his strenuous tolerance (limited to Protestants) may yet inspire. While one can easily see how Dr. Paul's own faith, his Congregationalism, and ecumenical mindedness would lead him to cast Cromwell's predicament this way, one may wonder whether Cromwell would have perceived it and spoken of it in the same fashion. Nevertheless, it is possible that Paul and not Cromwell may have reached the deeper level of understanding. A man may never perceive himself accurately, after all, because he cannot see himself in his true context.

A far less ecumenically minded point of view is that of Merle D'Aubigné, also a clergyman, and a notable historian of the Reformation. D'Aubigné perceived Cromwell as a part of the glorious rise and triumphant march of Protestantism. D'Aubigné's apparent prejudice against Roman Catholics may faithfully represent the popular prejudices of Cromwell's time. In this sense his bias may convey, in terms of attitude, the truth of the past more than it may distort it. The contrast between Paul and D'Aubigné emerges at this point. The former finds Cromwell involved in the universal problems of reconciling faith and activity; the latter champions Cromwell as the leader of the partisan Protestant interest against the reactionary Catholic cause.

Thomas Carlyle stands in sharp contrast to both Paul and D'Aubigné, for he was a secular historian and not a man of faith. Though without a religious faith, he was not without vision. He was the Evangelist of his own peculiar cult, hoping that England might be rescued from ugly industrializing and stifling democracy by an aristocracy of talent. Carlyle sketched Cromwell by the light of his own vision. He collected and published all the letters and speeches of Cromwell that he could find and linked these pieces together with a commentary of extraordinary brilliance and verve. For the first time, Cromwell's words were widely available to the public. That fact in itself did much to dispel the two centuries of doubt with which he had been regarded. Cromwell, as the excerpt from his speech shows, saw himself as God's special creature, buffeted by events. Carlyle, on the contrary, conceived of him as a dynamic creator of history, too humble to recognize or admit the real nature of his historic role. For Carlyle, Cromwell was a figure of destiny arisen to destroy the hollow era of royal and clerical control. He was bound to replace the old sham with a new reality, the empty form with solid substance, the earlier principle of government with the new principle of the rule of the best man. Carlyle had nothing but contempt for the masses, a contempt, we might add, that Cromwell did not share. For Carlyle, men of force who embraced the principle of an aristocracy of moral and intellectual, rather than social, quality were heroes and demigods. His history was unabashed hero-worship.

A more moderate, and still eminently readable, verdict came from John Buchan. In Buchan's biography the demigod becomes an ordinary country gentleman, enjoying mundane pleasures and drawing a robust sense of reality from the realities of his social background. Yet, in spite of his "ordinariness," Buchan accepted that Cromwell was a man born to rule and to rule undemocratically. Cromwell, he thought, was striving to establish the rule of the good in a rejuvenated state. This is similar to, though not identical with, the conception of Carlyle. No hero, Cromwell was nevertheless a great improvisor.

Quite another tack was taken by William C. Abbott, who, like Carlyle, gathered and reedited all the available Cromwell material. Unlike Carlyle, Abbott had an acute sense of the relativity of historical judgments. His essay canvasses the vagaries of past interpretations with an awareness that they have altered according to the new experiences of the historians rather than because of the emergence of new evidence from the past. Abbott embraced relativity himself, for he thought the rise of modern dictatorships had clarified Cromwell's place in history. "Dictatorship" aptly summed up the quality of the Protectorate. His view raises the question of the validity of historical analogies, not only between Cromwell and Hitler but also analogies in general.

Lord Macaulay had long since warned that historical analogies could be misleading in a review of Hallam's *Constitutional History of England* written in 1827. Hallam had paired Cromwell with Napoleon; Macaulay distinguished them, arguing that they differed because their circumstances differed.

Macaulay was the greatest of Whig historians, so it is fitting that his note be followed by a summation of Cromwell's statesmanship from a modern historian who stood in the Whig tradition. Sir Charles Firth never doubted Cromwell's integrity, emphasized his pragmatism, and laid the blame for the failure of his constitutional experiments on his honest concern for the Puritan minority. Firth also praised Cromwell for making progress possible in religious toleration, in unifying the British Isles, and in extending benevolent imperialism.

The assumption of progress was less surely held by John Morley. Morley was a practicing statesman, a close friend and supporter of Gladstone. The rise of imperialism and the difficulties in the way of solving the Irish problem bothered him. Unlike Firth, who wrote from the peace of the library, Morley had learned from experience how ephemeral political solutions could be. He was also less committed to the idea of the greatness of Imperial England. Yet Morley admired Cromwell because he crushed absolutism in Church and State. His rule served the function of a provisional keeping of the peace. Morley believed the English constitution had developed along lines which Cromwell would have disliked, and regarded him less as a modern than a medieval man: anti-parliamentary, anti-progressive, and unresponsive to public opinion.

Trevor-Roper is a more outspoken critic of Cromwell than Morley. With fine irony he describes Cromwell as backward not forward-looking. He was a politician who hoped to mimic Queen Elizabeth's love-tricks with her Parliaments yet who completely failed to understand how she had managed her Parliaments so skillfully. Cromwell's failures, however, stemmed not only from himself as an individual but also from the inadequate, unconstructive political outlook of his class. At this point, Trevor-Roper elaborates one of his distinctive contributions to discussion of the causes of the Civil War. His theme is that the war was brought on by the frustrations of the lesser country gentry, who had been left out of places of power and affluence through office-holding and court connections, and whose only desire was to destroy. Temperamentally unfit to build they could not transform their resentments into successful policies. Social changes and the stunted political mentality of the declining gentry explain Cromwell's pathetic failure as a statesman.

Like Trevor-Roper, though from a very different vantage, Christopher Hill has also been engaged for a long time in laying out the social origins of the English Revolution. In this essay, he is less concerned with passing judgment on Cromwell's success or failure as a statesman than in offering a viable explanation of the apparent complexity of the man. For Hill, Cromwell's career is rooted in his social situation. Cromwell is a paradox because his social situation was ambivalent. He was, on the one hand, a man who hesitated for long periods; yet, on the other hand, he was one who came to sudden swift decisions. Cromwell was a man of apparent hypocrisy yet patent sincerity, one who could extend the right hand of fellowship, but not the franchise, to low classes. He was a tolerant man, but a rabid anti-Catholic. Although linked through faith to lower and more radical groups, Cromwell was bound by interest and class to more conservative social elements.

John New takes up Hill's awareness of the paradoxical in Cromwell, linking Cromwell's behavior to the paradoxes of his Puritan faith. On the one hand, man is utterly fallen and depraved, yet on the other, he can be a member of a spiritualized church. Puritan metaphysics is dominated by the notion of grace and nature at once fused and also separated. The Puritan feared a severe last judgment yet was certain of heaven. He conceived of liberty as obedience, and thought of the moral law as being both hidden and revealed. New relates Cromwell's ambiguous behavior to these contradictory beliefs. His study raises the question of the relative influence of "bread and butter" factors or of ideology in forming behavior-patterns.

The last word should rest with S. R. Gardiner, the doyen of Victorian scholars of the early Stuart and Civil War periods. Gardiner's remark that Cromwell was a typical Englishman exemplifying typically English strengths and failings cannot easily be reconciled with Carlyle's or Abbott's view. Cromwell stands, Gardiner suggested, "to hold up a mirror to ourselves." One may not accept what seems to be implied: that English character was then and will remain the same. But in the special sense that historians tend to see their own interests reflected in their subject, Gardiner's phrase is plainly true. Yet, if there is carry-over from the present to the past, it may also be true that there is some carrying forward from the past to the present. Close examination to the evidence of the past may have helped to shape a historian's evaluation of the state and motives of man in general. While the quest for meaning implies that the historian does not disregard his preconceptions, it should also insure that his predispositions are tested and modified by the evidence. The pattern of sense which the historian seeks to impose on his material is a pattern that must fit both the evidence of the past and the individual student's sense of reality in the present. History should be reinterpretated not only by succeeding generations but also by each interested individual, for each can sound on the instrument of evidence a truth of different tone and sonority. Given a subject as baffling and enigmatic as Cromwell, and the complex nature of the historian's craft, it would be incredible and disappointing if only one cadence of truth emerged.

It may seem that objectivity is dethroned and bias made king. Fruitful questions, however, lie beyond the task of identifying and describing historians' idiosyncrasies. One can wonder what elements in a scholar's work cause others to admire and to value it, even though they may not accept the interpretation in whole or in part. This question leads to the recognition that there are levels of accuracy and gradations of mastery of the evidence. There are wide variations in style, and in the qualities of internal coherence and contemporary resonance. There are several depths of perception and degrees of originality. Measures of the conceptual grandeur, virtuosity, elegance, or aesthetic beauty in the patterning of evidence are unequal. There will always be greater or lesser strains between the more artistic of these norms and the demand for faithfulness. But, though many of these categories of judgment appear to be matters of taste, historians of radically different backgrounds and presuppositions frequently agree in their assessments of intellectual excellence. Where such agreement exists there flourishes the viable objectivity of the historical science. So Gardiner's plea is still relevant: we should strive to see Cromwell as a whole in the totality of his setting. The challenge yet remains to see Cromwell as he really was.

CHRONOLOGICAL TABLE

England at this time still used the Julian or Old Style calendar, whereas elsewhere in Europe the Gregorian or New Style calendar was in vogue. The English, old style ran 10 days ahead of the New Gregorian calendar; moreover it began the new year from March 25 instead of using the January 1 beginning of the new style. Historians tend to use the English dates used in England at the time, dating Cromwell's death for instance or his victories at Dunbar and Worcester on the 3rd rather than the 13th of September. But years are usually brought into conformity with the Gregorian calendar, and are assumed to have started on 1st of January.

1599	Cromwell's birth.
1603	Queen Elizabeth's death and James I's accession.
1603–4	Puritans' moderate reform demands rejected.
1605	Radical Puritans ejected from parishes.
1604–11	James' first Parliament meets in sessions of 1604, 1606–7 and 1610. Parliament proves to be far more assertive with regard to rights and privileges than earlier. Parliament fails to unite England and Scotland, and fails to work out an exchange of the Crown's vestigial feudal tax rights for a fixed Parliamentary subsidy.
1610	James introduces Bishops into Scotland without disturbing the structure of the Presbyterian system.
1616	James triumphs over the most independent-minded of the common law judges—Sir Edward Coke—who had wished to shield judges from royal pressure and interference, and who had argued that the King was subject to the law.
1618	Beginning of Thirty Years War on the Continent. Rise of the Duke of Buckingham, James' special favorite.

1620	Puritan pilgrims leave for New England.
1621–29	Ostensible reign of the Duke of Buckingham, who establishes his influence over Charles as well as James.
1621–25	Parliaments revive feudal procedure of impeachment to bring royal councillors to account. Francis Bacon, Lord Chancellor impeached in 1621 and the Lord Treasurer in 1624. Commons makes first steps to appropriation or ear-marking of supply in 1624. Attempts are made to influence Crown's marriage and foreign policies.
1625–	Feoffees for Impropriations set up to buy up tithe rights that had fallen into lay hands and use the proceeds to provide for and to place Puritan preachers in pulpits. James I dies (March) and Charles I succeeds. Rise of Laudian party in the Church.
1625–6	Parliament evidences distrust and distaste for Buckingham. Normally granted for the duration of a reign, tonnage and poundage is granted for one year only. Charles will continue to collect these customs and the law courts compel merchants to pay.
1627	Buckingham's expedition to relieve the beleaguered Huguenots on the Isle of Rhé is a failure to England's shame. Forced loans resisted.
1628–9	Cromwell elected to Parliament from Huntingdon. Petition of Right. Buckingham is assassinated by veteran of Isle of Rhé expedition. Londoners toast assassin in the streets.
1629	Parliament dissolves amid scenes of wild antipathy to the government.
1629–40 1630–	11 years tyranny or personal rule. New wave of Puritan migrations to New England. Continued Puritan activity and contact among future Parliamentary leaders in colonization companies. Conformity enforced in London and at Oxford under Laud.
1633	Foeffees for Impropriations expropriated, but Puritans in "lec-

tureships" continue to operate in London and other corporations. Laud becomes Archbishop of Canterbury.

1634   New financial expedients fashioned from old feudal rights of the crown; among them fines levied for infringing old forest laws (that is, old laws against disafforestation), and fines placed on those not taking out knighthood. Ship money levied on ports. Ship money levy extended to coastal and inland countries in 1635 and continued yearly until 1639. A test case is brought against the levy in 1637 by John Hampden, and the King's rights are upheld by a narrow majority of the bench, but thereafter ship money became almost unobtainable. Tonnage and poundage continued to be levied throughout this period.

1637   Public punishment and multilation of three leading Puritan critics of the Laudian Church.
New English, Laudian Prayer Book imposed on Scotish Church. Riot in St. Giles Cathedral, Edinburgh, develops into national resistance. A Covenant of opposition is circulated and subscribed. General Assembly of the Church of Scotland denounces Prayer Book and episcopacy.

1639   First "Bishops' War" against Scots ends in uneasy truce.

1640   Short Parliament refuses to vote taxes until grievances are debated, and so dissolved. Cromwell a member for Cambridge. Second "Bishops' War."
Long Parliament elected by November. Cromwell elected from Cambridge.

1640–42   Parliamentarians support a series of Acts striking down the men, the policies, and the institutional instruments or courts of "arbitrary" government.
In May, Cromwell urges destruction of episcopacy "root and branch." In November, 1641, an Irish rebellion raises the question of the control of the forces which would have to be raised to crush it.
Grand Remonstrance—or grand list—of grievances passed and published. Many moderate reformers begin to fear Puritan radicalism more than the Crown, and withdraw from opposition. Bishops impeached in December, and excluded by Act from the House of Lords early in 1642. Charles tries and fails to arrest five leading opponents in the House of Commons in January, 1642.

Militia ordinance does not win his assent. Pamphlet war follows until August, 1642, when King raises his standard. Cromwell raises troops of horse for Parliament.

1643   Scots sign Covenant with English against Charles.
In return for military aid, the Parliamentarians call an Assembly of Divines to settle a new form of religion for England. Fighting is inconclusive, though Cromwell is victorious in his battles and skirmishes.

1644–5   Cromwell helps organize the New Model Army, is made Lieutenant General, is instrumental in winning a decisive victory at the Battle of Naseby.

1646   As first civil war ends a modified form of Presbyterianism is set up.

1646–7   King negotiates with several parties. He comes too close to agreement with Parliamentary majority for Army's liking — Army intimidates Parliamentary majority. Famous debates held within the Army Council at Putney on the constitutional bases upon which the kingdom should be settled.

1647–8   King makes concessions to and an engagement with Scots, who henceforth support him against Parliamentary army. Second civil war begins. Cromwell fights Scots and Army purges English Parliament of moderate majority. Scots defeated at Preston in August, 1648. Cromwell enters Scotland.

1649   Cromwell returns briefly.
Charles I tried and executed in January. A Council of State and a Republic without a House of Lords are established. Cromwell subdues Ireland after victories and massacres at Drogheda and Wexford.

1650–1   Cromwell wins victories in Scotland at Dunbar (3rd of Sept., 1650, and at Worcester (3rd of Sept., 1651).

1653   Remnant or Rump of the Long Parliament dismissed by Cromwell. Republicans are permanently alienated.
A Parliament of Saints, or Nominated or Barebone's Parliament sits from July to December and ends after a moderate Puritan versus radical Puritan rift.

1654   Cromwell made Lord Protector. Commissions set up to monitor clergy, to place acceptable ministers and eject unacceptable clergy thereby creating a make-shift, broadly Independent church system. First Protectorate Parliament called on basis of a new franchise (on 3rd of Sept.) and dissolved (Jan., 1655) in the face of a dangerous alliance between republicans and Presbyterian, conservative parliamentary opponents.

1655–6   Rule of the Major Generals.

1656–7   Second Protectorate Parliament called. Draft of new constitution offering Cromwell the Crown is accepted without the title King. In the second session a Republican—Presbyterian opposition to the Protectorate, the loose church settlement, and the new House of Lords brings on a dissolution in Feb., 1658.

1658   Cromwell dies on 3rd of Sept.

1658–9   Brief Protectorate of Richard Cromwell, who shortly resigns.

1659–60   Rival factions in Parliament and Army vie for power. Civil anarchy.

1660   The English General, Monk, marches from Scotland to restore order in London. He communicates with Charles Stuart, calls the pre-purged Long Parliament together, who call a new "Convention" Parliament, which, in turn, recalls Charles II.

As the son of a King's cutler, JAMES HEATH (1629–64) was a staunch Royalist. He was made even stauncher by his being deprived of a studentship at Christ College, Oxford, by Parliamentary visitors in 1648. He spent the Interregnum in exile at the Hague with the court of Charles II and therefore did not know Cromwell. After the Restoration he worked as a proofreader and wrote popular chronicles of decidedly Royalist bias. His *Life . . . of Cromwell, the late Usurper* was one such piece. It was a popular biography that captured the Restoration mood of revulsion from the earlier Puritan period, and it became a potent source of misinformation for later historians who relied upon it. A brief extract is offered below to convey the flavor of the whole work and to represent a common view of Cromwell which lasted from the Restoration to the Victorian era.*

James Heath

Cromwell, the Usurper

This our Oliver Cromwell was son of Mr. Rob. Cromwell the third son of Sir Henry, a gentleman who went no less in esteem and reputation than any of his Ancestors, for his personal worth, till his unfortunate production of this his son and heir, whom he had by his wife Elizabeth Steward the niece of Sir Robert Steward, a gentleman of a competent fortune in that country, but of such a malign effect on the course of this his nephew's life, as hereafter shall be declared: that if all the lands he gave him, (as some were fenny ground) had been irrecoverably lost and deluged, by any accident or disaster whatsoever, it might have passed for a most propitious providential prevention of that dire mischief which that estate occasioned.

He was born April the 25th in St. Johns' Parish in the town of Huntingdon, and was christened in that church the 29th of the same month *anno domini* 1599 where Sir Oliver Cromwell his uncle gave him his name, being received into the bosom of the church by her rites and ceremonies, both [of] which he afterwards rent and tore, and ungraciously and impiously annulled and renounced.

From his infancy to his childhood he was of a cross and peevish disposition, which, being humoured by the fondness of his mother, made that rough and intractable temper more robust and outragious in his juvenile years, and adult and masterless at mans-estate.

No sooner therefore had he obtained the use of his tongue, but his father, care-

---

*From James Heath, *Flagellum: or the Life and Death, Birth and Burial of Oliver Cromwell, the late Usurper* (London, 1672), pp. 7–26. Text is modernised somewhat— Ed.

ful of his education, sent him to school to learn the elements of language and principals of religion; both which he studied with the same indifference, and faithlessness and fallacious endeavour, as afterwards appeared by his never speaking what he thought, nor believing what he heard, or was instructed in: so that his main policy was a radical and original hypocrisy, which growing up with him, could not but be [at] last after so many years of experience most exquisitly perfected.

From this a b c discipline and the slighted governance of a Mistress his father removed him to the tuition of Dr. Beard, schoolmaster of the free-school in that town: where his books began to persecute him, and learning to commence his great and irreconcilable enemy; for his master honestly and severely observing that, and others his faults (which like weeds, sprung out of his rank and uncultivable nature), did by correction hope to better his manners; and with a diligent hand and careful eye to hinder the thick growth of those vices, which were so predominant and visible in him: yet though herein he trespassed upon that respect and lenity due and usual to children of his birth and quality; he prevailed nothing against his obstinate and perverse inclination. The learning and civility he had, coming upon him like fits of enthusiasm, now a hard student for a week or two, and then a truant . . . for twice as many months of no settled constancy; [remained] the very tenor and mode of his future life till his grand attainment.

Amongst the rest of those ill qualities which fructuated in him at this age, he was very notorious for robbing of orchards; a crime and an ordinary trespass, but grown so scandalous and in by the frequent spoils and damages of trees, breaking of hedges and inclosures, committed by this apple-dragon, that many solemn complaints were made both to his father and Master for redress thereof; which missed not their satisfaction and expiation out of his hide, on which so much pains were lost, that, that very offence ripened in him afterwards to the throwing down of all boundaries of law or conscience, and the stealing and tasting of the forbidden fruit of sovereignty, by which (as the serpent told him) he should be like unto a God.

From this, he passed unto another more manly theft, the robbing of dove-houses, stealing the young pigeons, and eating and merchandizing of them; and that so publicly, that he became dreadfully suspect to all the adjacent country. And this was an unhappy allusory omen of his after actions, when he robbed the King his sovereign of his innocence and virtues, and prostituted them to the people and soldiery and made the world about him afraid of his villanies.

It was at this time of his adolescency, that he dreamed, or a familiar rather instincted him and put it into his head, that he should be king of England; for it cannot be conceived, that now there should be any such near resemblance of truth in dreams and divinations (besides the confidence, with which he repeated it, and the difficulty to make him forget the arrogant conceit and opinionated pride he had of himself, it was some impulse of a spirit) since they have ceased long ago. However the vision came, most certain it is, that his father was exceedingly troubled at it; and having angerly rebuked him for the vanity, idleness, and impudence thereof; and seeing him yet persist in the same presumption caused Dr. Beard to whip him for it; which was done to no more purpose than the rest of his chastisements, his scholar growing insolent and incorrigible from those results and swasions within him, to which all other dictates and instructions were useless, and as a dead letter.

Now to confirm this royal humour the more in his ambitious and vain-glorious brain, it happened (as it was then generally the custome in all great free schools) [that] a play called *The Five Senses,* was to be acted by the scholars of this school, and Oliver Cromwell, as a confident youth, was named to act the part of Tactus, the sense of feeling; in the personation of which as he came out of the attiring room upon the stage, his head encircled with a chaplet of laurel, he stumbled at a crown, purposely laid there, which stooping down he took up, and crowned himself therewithal, adding beyond his cue, some majestical mighty words; and with this passage also the event of his life held good analogy and proportion, when he changed the laurel of his victories (in the late unnatural war) to all the power, authority, and splendor that can be imagined within the compass of a crown.

Nevertheless the relation of a father, and one so stern and strict an examiner of him, (he being in his own nature of a difficult disposition, and great spirit, and one that would have due distances observed towards him from all persons, which began his reverence for the country-people) kept him in some awe and subjection, till his translation to Cambridge; where he was placed in Sydney [Sussex] College, more to satisfy his father's curiosity and desire, than out of any hopes of completing him in his studies, which never reached any good knowledge of the Latin tongue.

During his short residence here, where he was more famous for his exercises in the fields than in the schools, (in which he never had the honour of because no worth or merit to, a degree) being one of the chief match-makers and players at football, cudgels, or any other boisterous sport or game; his father Mr. Robert Cromwell died, leaving him to the scope of his own inordinate and irregular will, swayed by the bent of very violent and strong passions.

There is little to be said more of his father, that is requisite to his son's story, further than this, that whereas it was reported Oliver kept a brew-house, that is a mistake; for the brew-house was kept in his father's time, and managed by his mother and his father's servants, without any concernment of either of these therein, the accounts being always given to the Mistress, who after her husband's death, did continue in the same employment and calling of a brewer, and thought it no disparagement to sustain the estate and port of a younger brother, as Mr. Robert Cromwell was, by those lawful means; however, not so reputable as other gains and trades are accounted.

It was not long after his death, Oliver, e'er weary of the muses, and, that strict course of life (though he gave latitude enough to it in his wild sallies and flying out) abandoned the University, and returned home, saluted with the name of young Mr. Cromwell, now in the room and place of his father, which how he became, his uncontrolled debaucheries did publicly declare, for drinking, wenching, and the like outrages of licentious youth, none so infamed as this young Tarquin, who would not be contraried in his lusts, in the very strain and to the excess of that regal ravisher [the Devil?].

These pranks made his mother advise with herself and his friends, what she should do with him, to remove the scandal which had been cast upon the family by his means; and therefore it was concluded to send him to one of the inns of court, under pretence of his studying the laws; where among the mass of people in London, and frequency of vices of all sorts, his might pass in the throng, without that particular near reflection upon his relations, and at worst the infamy should stick only on himself.

Lincolns-Inns was the place pitched upon, and Mr. Cromwell in a suitable garb to his fortunes was sent, where but for a very little while he continued, for the nature of the place and the studies there, were so far regretful beyond all his tedious apprenticeship to the more facile academic sciences, (by reason laws were the bar and obstacle of his impetuous resolutions, and the quite contrary to his loose and libertine spirit) that he had a kind of antipathy to his company and converse there; and so spent his time in an inward spite, which for that space superseded the enormous extravagancy of his former viciousness. His vices having a certain kind of intermission, succession, or transmigration, like a complete revolution of wickedness into one another, so that few of his feats were practised here: and it is some kind of good luck for that honourable society, that he left so small and so innocent a memorial of his membership therein.

His next traverse was back again into the country to his mother, and there he fell to his old trade, and frequented his old haunts, consumed his money in tipling, and then ran on score perforce: in his drink he used to be so quarrelsome as (few unless as mad as himself) durst keep him company; his chief weapon in which he delighted, and at which he fought several times with tinkers, pedlers, and the like (who most an eve go armed therewith) was a quarterstaff; in which he was so skillful, that seldom did any overmatch him. A boisterous discipline and rudiment of his martial skill and valour, which with so much fierceness he manifested afterward in the ensuing war.

These and the like strange, wild, and dishonest actions, made him everywhere a shame or a terror; insomuch that the ale-wives of Huntingdon and other places, when they saw him coming would use to cry out to one another, "Here comes young Cromwell, shut up your doves:" for he made it no punctilio to invite his roisters to a barrel of drinks and give it them at the charge of his host, and in satisfaction thereof either beat him, or break his windows, if he offered any stew, or gave any look or sign of refusal or discontent.

His lustful wantonnesses were not less predominant than the other unruly appetites of his mind; that there might no vice be wanting to make his life a system of iniquity; the public, open and more ingenious vilenesses of his youth, becoming the several dangerous and cruel villanies of his old age, it being now his rude custom, to seize upon all women he met in his way on the road, and perforce ravish a kiss, or some lewder satisfaction from them; and if any resistance were made by their company, then to vindicate and allay this violence and heat of his blood, with the letting out of theirs, whose defence of their friends' honour, and chastity, innocently engaged them. And the same riots was he guilty of against any who would not give him the way; so that he was a rebel in manners, long before he was a Belial in policy.

I am loath to be too large in such particulars, which may render me suspect of belying him, out of prejudice or revenge; but I have heard it confirmed so often from knowing persons, and the stories made sue of by his party, who did thereby magnify his conversion, making him thus dear and precious unto God, that I was obliged to mention them, partly as due to the memoir of him, which pretends to an exact biography, as well in the minute and small beginnings, as in the grand and most important events of his life; and partly to set him as a remark against all satanical delusions of instantaneous sanctity; with which yet at this very day the world is bewitched, though they have seen in him the tragical, and even diabolical effects of his religious austerity.

Only one thing I may not omit; by these lewd actions he had so alienated the affections of his uncle and godfather Sir Oliver Cromwell, that he could not endure the sight of him, having in his own presence in the great hall of his house, where he magnificently treated King James, at his assumption to the crown of England, in a Christmas time, (which was always highly observed by him by feasting, and keeping open house) played this unhandsome and unseemly trick or frolic; with the relation of which the reader will be pleased to indulge me, because I have seen it recounted by a worthy and learned hand.

It was Sir Oliver's custom in that festival, to entertain in his house a master of mis-rule or the revels, to make mirth for the guests, and to direct the dances and the music, and generally all manner of sports and gambols; this fellow, Mr. Cromwell having besmeared his own clothes and hands with surreverence, accosts [him] in the midst of a frisking dance, and so grimed him and others upon every turn, that such a stink was raised, that the spectators could hardly endure the room; whereupon the said master of mis-rule perceiving the matter, caused him to be laid hold on, and by his command to be thrown into a pond adjoining the house, and there to be sowsed over head and ears, and rinsed of the faith and pollution sticking to him; which was accordingly executed, Sir Oliver suffering his nephew to undergo the punishment of his unmannerly folly.

By this time, and by these ways Oliver had run himself out of that patrimony he had, and brought his mother to the same

near ruin; when taking a sad prospect, from the brink of this destruction, of his present desperate condition, a giddy inspiration seized him, and all of a sudden so seemed to change and invert him, that he now became the wonder, who just before was the hissing, and scorn of all people. And that this conversion might seem true and real, he manifested it with the publican first in the temple, (the church) which he devoutly and constantly frequented, affecting the companies and discourses of orthodox divines, no way given to that schism of non-conformity; into which Oliver soon after fell, not out of seduction and ignorance, but sedition, and malice, and treasonable design.

But this appearance of such a reformation in him (as he no doubt forecast it) did effectually conduce to his present purpose; for these reverend divines, glad of the return of this prodigal, made it their business to have him received and welcomed with the fatted calf, to remove the prejudices that lie upon the objected narrowness of Christianity: and therefore severally and jointly they deal with Sir Robert Steward, his uncle (for Sir Oliver would by no means hear of him, as being assured and confirmed against him out of some good hints certainly of his own observation) to take him into his favour, and did at last prevail so upon him, that he declared him his heir, and, dying soon after, left him an estate of four or five hundred pounds a year; which being got and obtained by so impious practice, a kind of inverted simony, to purchase lands by counterfeit gifts and graces, could not escape the canker of sacrilege; but in few years moulded away piecemeal, nothing at all remaining thereof but a thached house, with some lands of forty or fifty pounds a year, in a town called Wells, within four miles of Wisbech in the Isle of Ely.

In the interval of this estate, having

served himself of those venerable divines, he fell in with some of the preciser sort; began to shew himself at lectures, to entertain such preachers at his house, in countenance that way, and be very zealous in all meetings of such people, which then began to be frequent and numerous; and to exercise with them by praying and the like; to estrange himself from those his benefactors; and at last to appear a public dissenter from the discipline of the church of England. He had matched, a little before, upon the account of this estate, in reversion, with a kinswoman of Mr. Hampden's, and Mr. Goodwin's of Buckinghamshire, by the name of Elizabeth, daughter of one Sir James Bowcher, who he trained up and made the waiting woman of his providences, and lady-rampant of his successful greatness, which she personated afterwards as imperiously as himself; so did the incubus of his bed make her partaker too in the pleasures of the throne. These men eminent for puritanism, together with their preachers set him up as the prime man of his county, for religion, integrity, and true godliness.

But his estate still decaying, he betook himself at last to a farm, being parcel of the royalty of St. Ives; where he intended to husband it, and try what could be done by endeavour, since nothing (as yet succeded by design: and accordingly, took servants, and bought him all utensils and materials, and ploughs, carts and the better to prosper his own and his men's labour, every morning before they stirred out, the family was called together to prayers, at which exercise, very often, they continued so long, that it was nine of the clock in the morning before they began their work; which awkward beginning of their labour sorted with a very sorry issue; for the effect of those prayers was, that the hands and plowmen seeing this zeal of their master, which dispensed with the profitable and most commodious part of the day for their labour, thought they might borrow the other part for their pleasure; and therefore commonly they went to plough with a pack of cards in their pockets, and having turned up two or three furrows, set themselves down to game till dinner time; when they returned to the second part of their devotion, and measured out a good part of the afternoon with dinner, and a repetition of some market lecture that had been preached the day before. And that little work that was done, was done so negligently and by halves, that scarce half a crop ever reared it self upon his grounds; so that he was (after five years time) glad to abandon it, and get a friend of his to be the tenant for the remainder of his time.

During his continuance here, he was grown (that is pretended to be) so just, and of so scrupulous a conscience, that having some years before won thirty pounds of one Mr. Calton at play, meeting him accidentally, he desired him to come home with him and to receive his money, telling him that he had got it by indirect and unlawful means, and that it would be a sin in him to detain it any longer; and did really pay the gentleman the said thirty pounds back again.

Now was he therefore thinking of transporting himself and his family into New England, a receptacle of the puritan, who flocked thither amain, for liberty of conscience: but he [especially], for that his purse and credit were so exhausted that he could no longer stay here. Which resolution he had taken up before the estate of his uncle fell to him, and was put aside it, by the amplitude of that fortune to maintain him here: and that a last (though wasted and gone) rendered him a candidate for the ensuing parliament, and supplied him before with the ability of disbursing £500 upon account of Irish adventures towards the settling a plantation in Ulster, in the Kingdom.

Yet was this the very last remains of that accessional inheritance, he being forced to borrow in town here very precariously and by the mediation of friends (though no greater sum than ten pounds), (nay formerly ten shillings were acceptable) at several times, which he received with this inducing expression; that though sometime he had made no conscience of repaying any money, yet he would punctually now keep his word: which indeed he did justly observe; and this an eminent citizen his friend and school fellow had often declared. The last sum he borrowed being very anxiously besought and entreated, as rising to a £100 which upon his growing greatness pleasured him, and was most abusefully employed in hiring wagons for the Earl of Essex's army, then advancing against the King. To this constant and insuperable indigency and ebb of forturne was he kept and decreed to the brink of our troubles, that his ruins and private misery might the more industriously force him to the reparation of them, by the public calamities, and then carry him to the mixed affluence and excess of wealth and state-usurpation.

In this new conversation and change, he was grown so cunning, as to comply with those silent modes of kindness and private conveyances of friendship, which imported him a great deal more than he exported, for he was very much in the esteem of the best of the faction.

Nor did he omit any other duty or civility, or office of love to any especially to those of the household, as they then termed the people of the separation; insomuch that he had screwed himself into the affections of many well-meaning people, whose assistance he obtained against his use for it in his election to the Long Parliament; of which [more] presently.

He was a great stickler likewise against Ship-money, in which danger his great friend and patron Mr. Hampden was so far embarked: nor was he better affected to the Scotch war, then growing on, as he to his hazard discovered himself to some chief commanders of the English army, who in their march against the Scots quartered at his house; which discourses drawing suspicion upon him, made him the more popular in those parts which were generally infected with puritanism.

About the same time on Mr. Bernard's coming to be Recorder of the town of Huntingdon, some difference about precedency of place happened between them, (Oliver's spirit being too high to yield to any person in that town, where his family had continued of the best rank some years together) and therefore to avoid the cession of his honour to another, he withdrew himself into the Isle of Ely, where he more frequently and publicly owned himself a teacher, and did preach in other men's as well as in his own house, according as the brotherhood agreed and appointed.

While he continued here in this fashion, there were discourses of new writs issuing out for the parliament in 1640, and about the same time or a little before, it was the hap[penstance] of one Richard Tims since Alderman of Cambridge, and a man generally known throughout all the late times, having sat in all the functions thereof, to be at a conventicle, (as he usually every Sunday rode to the Isle of Ely to that purpose, having a brother who entertained them in his course) where he heard this Oliver, with such admiration, that he thought there was not such a precious man in the nation; and took such a liking to him, that from that time he did nothing, but ruminate and meditate on the man and his gifts.

And by this slender wire was such an

engine moved, that afterwards tore up the church and state; that the reader will perceive his solicitous busy fate cast always about to compass her design of his advancement; and all by such uncouth and strange passes, such unexpected and ungoverned contingency of things, that she had left him as the only example, whom by the meanest offices and artifices and pragmatic insinuations she ever raised to any such sublimity.

For this Richard Tims before the writs were issued out (in which time he had opportunity of hearing Oliver once and again) began to hammer in his head a project of getting him chosen a burgess for Cambridge, himself being then but one of the 24. With this device he presently repaired to one Mr. Wildbore a draper, a kinsman of Cromwell and a non-conformist likewise; and after some commendatory language of Oliver, propounded to him the choosing of him burgess; to which Wildbore answered that it was impossible, because he was no freeman of the town.

This almost dashed the project: notwithstanding as he was returning home, his mind gave him to ask the advice of his neighbour Ibbot a tallow chandler, whom he found working in his frock, and who gave him the same answer: and thereupon Tims concluded to forecease the design, and departed. But before he was far from the house, Ibbot, hankering after the business, had thought of an expedient, and caused him to be called back, when he told him, that the Mayor had power to make a freeman, and saith he, you know Mr. Kitchinman the attorney (who was a puritan likewise) he and the Mayor have married two sisters; it is possible he may persuade his brother to confer his freedom upon Mr. Cromwell, and to that purpose you, and I, and Mr. Wildbore will go to Mr. Kitchinman's

presently, and speak to him about the business, but the Mayor must not know the reason and design of it; for he is a perfect royalist.

Accordingly they three went to Kitchinman's, laid open the worth of Cromwell, and easily engaged him in the plot; the same night he went to the Mayor's, by name Alderman French, and finding him at supper, without more ado acquainted him with his business, told him that one Mr. Cromwell had a mind to come and dwell in the town, but first he would be made a freeman, that he was a deserving gentleman, and that he would be an honour and support to the town, which was full of poor; and many more good morrows: to which the Mayor answered that he was sorry he could not comply with his desires, for he had engaged his freedom already to the King's fisherman, and could not recede from his word; whereto Kitchinman presently replied, brother, do you give your freedom to Mr. Cromwell, I will warrant and take upon me what the town shall give a freedom to the said fisherman, and with some other words persuaded the unwary Mayor to consent.

All this while Cromwell was utterly ignorant what had been transacted at Cambridge, but now Tims sent him word, that in order to make him a Burgess, he with his party has procured a freedom from the Mayor; that therefore he should not fail to be there the next court day. This message Cromwell received with a like gladness and wonder, and not to be wanting to the industry and zeal of the faction, came privately to Cambridge the day before, and took up his lodging at one Almond's, a grocer.

Next day the court being sat, the Mayor rose up, as the manner is, and declaring that he had conferred his freedom upon a right worthy gentleman, Mr. Cromwell, using the same character of him which he had received from Kitchinman, and hereupon a mace was sent to bring Cromwell into the court, who came thither in a scarlet coat laid with a broad gold lace, and was there seated, then sworn and saluted by the Mayor, Aldermen, and the rest with, welcome brother. In the meanwhile Cromwell had caused a good quantity of wine to be brought into the town house, (with some confectionary stuff) which was liberally filled out, and as liberally taken off, to the warming of most of their noddles; when Tims and the other three spread themselves among the company, and whispered into the ears, would not this man make a brave Burgess for the ensuing Parliament? Which being instilled, with the merry juice *gratis* and plentifully given them, could not but have a kind operation in the next occasion: and a fortnight after another common hall was called for the said election of Burgesses, where was first named Mr. Lowry, who carried it by the general suffrage, after him one Mr. Mutis a councellor, and he had the votes of a great many, all of them royalists; lastly our Oliver was named, and the faction bawled as if they were mad, and by plurality of voices carried it clear from Mr. Mutis.

When the Mayor now perceived the jig, and how Kitchinman had fooled him, he could have pulled the hair off his head: but the thing was remediless, he was legally chosen; for the faction had brought men thither, that had left off their gowns for 30 years together. In the meanwhile the zealots triumphed that they had got such a champion, and indulged their bellies at his cost, most of which he borrowed, while by this means the kingdom had one viper more fostered, to the exenterating of her bowels . . .

Having now attained his desire and aims, which was to help to blow up those coals of dissention and rage, which had kindled in the breast of his malcontent party so long, and now were like to have free vent to the setting the kingdoms into a conflagration; like a right incendiary, where he found any grievance complained of, he would make himself a party concerned in it, enquire into the number of strength of the faction that managed the complaint, offer his and his friends' assistance, encourage them to clamour against the mal-administration, and generally set afoot those mischievous petitions, which were brought thick and threefold to the Parliament; till his faction had so exasperated the King against them, that there seemed no possibility of reconciling them, making even all the King's most earnest endeavors for an accommodation, arguments of refusing it. And though at first he was none of the principal of the cabal, being taken in and tutored by Mr. Pym and Hampden, (as finding him of a bold and undertaking spirit of what mischief soever was propounded to him) yet was he notably and highly instrumental and subservient to the conspiracy; and at last arose to such a knowledge and capacity of the mystery, that he scorned their puny rudiments, when with a deeper atheism he set up for himself.

The determinate time was now come, for which the cabal of the puritan had so long laboured; and that none of those things which had been so direfully prophesied of their schism (if it ever should attain any power or prevalency) might want, or rather not exceed belief; the whole kingdom of a sudden, as if some magical charm had transformed the state and shape of it, seemed rather a scene or boscage of wild and brutal creatures, than a governed or civil community. But because this particular has been so largely treated of, and is yet fresh in memory, and will hardly ever be forgotten; it will not be much material to urge it further unless to the maintenance of this maxim; that the uproars and rebellions of subjects, upon what pretense soever, do always end in the greatest tyrannies, and turn to their most unsufferable and ignominious miseries; and that their darling demagogues, whom with applauses and arms they have shouldered up, and have reared and exalted above the reach of the law, make it no nicety afterwards to trample upon the necks of their raisers; and to swim in their blood, whose itching swelled their ambition to the throne.

Son of a Parliamentarian, EDMUND LUDLOW (1617–1692) became a convinced republican in the last years of the Long Parliament. He remained a republican throughout the Protectorate and throughout a precarious exile in Switzerland after the Restoration. As a dashing military commander and a devout Puritan, Ludlow had much in common with Cromwell. He came to believe, however, that Oliver had deceitfully betrayed the "good old cause" to satisfy his personal ambition. His *Memoirs,* written in exile, are both a history and an autobiography. They show that Cromwell was subject to the same charge from the left that was levied from the right.*

Edmund Ludlow

Festering Ambition

General Cromwell had long been suspected by wise and good men; but he had taken such care to form and mould the army to his humour and interests, that he had filled all places either with his own creatures, or with such as hoped to share with him in the sovereignty, and removed those who foreseeing his design, had either the courage or honesty to oppose him in it. His pernicious intentions did not discover themselves openly till after the battle at Worcester, which in one of his letters to the Parliament he called The Crowning Victory. . . . In a word, so much was he elevated with that success, that Mr. Hugh Peters,† as

he since told me, took so much notice of it, as to say in confidence to a friend upon the road in his return from Worcester, that Cromwell would make himself king. He now began to despise divers members of the House whom he had formerly courted, and grew most familiar with those whom he used to shew most aversion to . . .

When the time appointed for the meeting of this assembly was come,‡ Cromwell went in a coach to Westminster, accompanied by his horse and foot guard, with many officers of the army on foot; where being arrived, his first business was to appear in his kingly garb at the Abby, there to hear a sermon with the

---
†At this time (1651 chaplain to the Council of State — Ed.

‡The first Protectorate Parliament — Ed.

---
*From Edmund Ludlow, *The Memoirs of Edmund Ludlow, 1625–1672,* ed. C. H. Firth, 2 vols. (Oxford, 1896) I, 344, 390; II, 8–9. Used by permission of the publishers, Clarendon Press, Oxford.

members of that assembly before they went about their other affairs. Which done, he went into the Painted Chamber, where he entertained the members with a tedious speech, wherein he endeavoured to make it appear, that things were brought to this pass, not by his contrivance, but by the over-ruling hand of God; assuring them, that he was much rejoiced to see so free an assembly of the people met together, and that he resolved to submit himself to their judgment. But notwithstanding these specious pretences, he caused the Lord Grey of Grooby, Mr. John Wildman, Mr. Highland, and others, who had always manifested a constant affection to the Commonwealth, to be excluded from the House . . .

About the same time Mr. Peters, who still kept fair with those at Whitehall, made me a visit; and in our conversation about the public affairs I freely told him my opinion concerning the actions of Cromwell, endeavouring to make him sensible not only of his injustice, but great imprudence, thus to sacrifice the common cause to his ambition, and by every step he had lately taken to strengthen the hands of the common enemy, whereby he would undoubtedly open a way for the return of the family of the late king, who would not fail to do all that revenge could inspire them with: whereas if he had made use of his power to establish the just liberties of the nation, or could yet be persuaded so to do, he might live more honoured and esteemed, have the pleasure and satisfaction arising from so generous an action when he died, and leave his own family, together with the whole body of the people, in a most happy and flourishing condition. He confessed that what I had said was most true, but added, that there was not a man about him who had courage enough to tell him so: that for his part he had observed him immediately after the victory at Worcester to be so elevated, that he then began to fear what was since come to pass; and that he told a friend with whom he then quartered in his return to London, that he was inclined to believe Cromwell would endeavour to make himself king.

The usurper having governed as he thought long enough by virtue of the Instrument of Government, which tho drawn up by himself and his creatures, was now thought to lay too great a restraint upon his ambitious spirit; and resolving to rest satisfied with nothing less than the succession of his family to the Crown, he attempted to make himself king. To this end he thought it necessary to call [another] Parliament.

OLIVER CROMWELL (1599–1658) delivered this speech in 1654 to the first Parliament assembled since he had assumed the title "Lord Protector" under the new constitution called the Instrument of Government. Parliament had been sitting a week. Although called in accordance with the terms of the Instrument, the members, led by the republicans, were eager to alter it in fundamental as well as incidental ways. So Cromwell spoke to justify his own position, to lay to rest attacks upon his integrity if he could, and to call a halt to constitution-tampering. Above all, he wished to make quite clear his role in the final dissolution of the Long Parliament and his position at the time of the resignation of members of the Parliament of Saints. Instead of futile debate, he wanted Parliament to settle real grievances and heal the rifts in the nation. Is his justification convincing?*

The second part of the selection below is taken from a speech to a committee of his second Protectorate Parliament in 1657. A new constitution had been drafted in which he was named King. After long deliberation he refused the kingship. Does his reasoning throw light upon his motives?**

Oliver Cromwell

Self-justification

I see it will be necessary for me now a little to magnify my office, which I have not been apt to do. I have been of this mind, I have been always of this mind, since first I entered upon it, that if God will not bear it up, let it sink! But if a duty be incumbent upon me to bear my testimony unto it, (which in modesty I have hitherto forborne,) I am in some measure now necessitated thereunto. And therefore that will be the prologue to my discourse.

I called not myself to this place. I say again, I called not myself to this place; of that, God is witness. And I have many witnesses who, I do believe, could readily lay down their lives to bear witness to the truth of that, that is to say, that I called not myself to this place. And being in it, I bear not witness to myself; but God and the people of these nations have borne testimony to it also.

If my calling be from God, and my testimony from the people, God and

*From W. C. Abbott, *The Writings and Speeches of Oliver Cromwell,* 4 vols. (Cambridge, Mass., 1937–47) III, 452–456. Used by permission of the President and Fellows of Harvard College and Harvard University Press, Cambridge, Mass.

**The second section is taken from Thomas Carlyle, *Oliver Cromwell's Letters and Speeches,* 3 vols, in one, (London, 1888), III, 249–254.

the people shall take it from me, else I will not part with it. I should be false to the trust that God hath placed upon me, and to the interest of the people of these nations, if I should.

That I called not myself to this place, is my first assertion.

That I bear not witness to myself, but have many witnesses, is my second.

These are the two things I shall take the liberty to speak more fully to you of.

To make plain and clear that which I have said, I must take liberty to look back.

I was by birth a gentleman, living neither in any considerable height, nor yet in obscurity. I have been called to several employments in the nation—to serve in Parliaments—and (because I would not be over tedious) I did endeavour to discharge the duty of an honest man in those services, to God, and His people's interest, and of the Commonwealth; having, when time was, a competent acceptation in the hearts of men, and some evidences thereof. I resolve not to recite the times and occasions and opportunities that have been appointed me by God to serve him in, nor the presence and blessing of God bearing then testimony to me.

I, having had some occasions to see (together with my brethren and countrymen) a happy period put to our sharp wars and contests with the then common enemy, hoped, in a private capacity, to have reaped the fruit and benefit, together with my brethren, of our hard labours and hazards: to wit, the enjoyment of peace and liberty, and the privileges of a Christian and of a man, in some equality with others, according as it should please the Lord to dispense unto me.

And when, I say, God had put an end to our wars, at least brought them to a very hopeful issue, very near an end

(after Worcester fight) I came up to London to pay my service and duty to the Parliament that then sat. And hoping that all minds would have been disposed to answer that which seemed to be the mind of God, (*viz.*) to give peace and rest to His people, and especially to those who had bled more than others in the carrying on of the military affairs, I was much disappointed of my expectation, for the issue did not prove so. Whatever may be boasted or misrepresented, it was not so, nor so.

I can say in the simplicity of my soul, I love not, I love not (I declined it in my former speech) I say I love not to rake into sores or to discover nakednesses. That which I drive at is this; I say to you, I hoped to have had leave to have retired to a private life. I begged to be dismissed of my charge; I begged it again and again. And God be judge between me and all men if I lie in this matter! That I lie not in matter of fact is known to very many; but whether I tell a lie in my heart, as labouring to represent to you that which was not upon my heart, I say, the Lord be judge. Let uncharitable men, that measure others by themselves, judge as they please; as to the matter of fact, I say it is true. As to the ingenuity and integrity of my heart in that desire, I do appeal as before upon the truth of that also. But I could not obtain what my soul longed for, and the plain truth is I did afterwards apprehend that some did think (my judgment not suiting with theirs) that it could not well be. But this, I say to you, was between God and my soul, between me and that assembly.

I confess I am in some strait to say what I could say, and what is true of what then followed.

I pressed the Parliament,† as a member, to period themselves, once, and again,

_____
† The Rump of the Long Parliament—Ed.

and again, and ten and twenty times over. I told them (for I knew it better than any one man in the Parliament could know it, because of my manner of life, which was to run up and down the nation, and so might see and know the temper and spirits of all men, the best of men) that the nation loathed their sitting; I knew it. And, so far as I could discern, when they were dissolved, there was not so much as the barking of a dog, or any general and visible repining at it. You are not a few here present that can assert this as well as myself.

And that there was high cause for their dissolving is most evident, not only in regard there was a just fear of the Parliaments perpetuating themselves, but because it was their design. And had not their heels been trod upon by importunities from abroad, even to threats, I believe there would never have been thoughts of rising or of going out of that room to the world's end.

I myself was sounded, and by no mean persons tempted, and addresses were made to me to that very end, that it might have been thus perpetuated, that the vacant places might be supplied by new elections, and so continue from generation to generation.

I have declined, I have declined very much, to open these things to you; yet having proceeded thus far, I must tell you that poor men under this arbitrary power were driven like flocks of sheep by forty in a morning, to the confiscation of goods and estates, without any man being able to give a reason that two of them had deserved to forfeit a shilling. I tell you the truth. And my soul, and many persons whose faces I see in this place, were exceedingly grieved at these things, and knew not which way to help it, but by their mournings and giving their negatives when occasions served.

I have given you but a taste of miscarriages; I am confident you have had opportunities to hear much more of them, for nothing is more obvious. It's true, this will be said, that there was a remedy to put an end to this perpetual Parliament endeavoured, by having a future Representative. How it was gotten, and by what importunities that was obtained, and how unwillingly yielded unto, is well known.

What was this remedy? It was a seeming willingness to have successive Parliaments. What was that succession? It was, that when one Parliament had left their seat, another was to sit down immediately in the room thereof, without any caution to avoid that which was the danger, (viz.) perpetuating of the same Parliaments; which is a sore now that will ever be running, so long as men are ambitious and troublesome, if a due remedy be not found. So then, what was the business? It was a conversion from a Parliament that should have been and was perpetual, to a Legislative Power always sitting; & so the liberties, and interests, and lives of people not judged by any certain known laws and power, but by an arbitrary power—which is incident and necessary to Parliaments—by an arbitrary power, I say, to make men's estates liable to confiscation, and their persons to imprisonments, sometimes by laws made after the fact committed, often by taking the judgment both in capital and criminal things to themselves, who in former times were not known to exercise such a judicature.

This I suppose was the case, and in my opinion the remedy was fitted to the disease, especially coming in the rear of a Parliament so exercising the power and authority as this had done but immediately before.

Truly I confess, upon these grounds,

and with the satisfaction of divers other persons, seeing nothing could be had otherwise, that Parliament was dissolved. We, desiring to see if a few might have been called together for some short time, who might put the nation into some way of certain settlement, did call those gentlemen out of the several parts of the nation for that purpose.†

And as I have appealed to God before you already, I know (and I hope I may say it) though it be a tender thing to make appeals to God, yet in such exigencies as these I trust it will not offend His Majesty, especially to make them before persons that know God, and know what conscience is, and what it is to lie before the Lord, I say that, as a principal end in calling that assembly was the settlement of the nation, so a chief end to myself was that I might have opportunity to lay down the power that was in my hands. I say to you again, in the presence of that God who hath blessed and been with me in all my adversities and successes, that was, as to myself, my greatest end. A desire perhaps (and I am afraid) sinful enough to be quit of the power God had most providentially put into my hand, before he called for it, and before those honest ends of our fighting were attained and settled. I say, the authority I had in my hand being so boundless as it was, I being by Act of Parliament General of all the forces in the three nations of England, Scotland, and Ireland (in which unlimited condition I did not desire to live a day,) did call that meeting for the ends before expressed.

What the event and issue of that meeting was, we may sadly remember: it hath much teaching in it, and I hope will make us all wiser for the future.

†The Parliament of the Saints or Barebones Parliament—Ed.

But this meeting [not] succeeding, as I have formerly said to you, and giving such a disappointment to our hopes, I shall not now make any repetition thereof. Only the effect was, that they came and brought to me a parchment, signed by very much the major part of them, expressing their resigning and redelivery of the power and authority that was committed to them back again into my hands. And I can say it in the presence of divers persons here, that do know whether I lie in that, that I did not know one tittle of that resignation, until they all came and brought it, and delivered it into my hands; of this there are also in this presence many witnesses.

I received this resignation, having formerly used my endeavours and persuasions to keep them together. Observing their differences, I thought it my duty to give advices to them, that so I might prevail with them for union, but it had the effect that I told you, and I had my disappointment.

When this was so, we were exceedingly to seek how to settle things for the future. My power again by this resignation was as boundless and unlimited as before; all things being subjected to arbitrariness, and [myself] a person having power over the three nations boundlessly and unlimited, and upon the matter, all government dissolved, all civil administrations at an end, as will presently be made [to] appear.

The gentlemen that undertook to frame this government did consult divers days together, (they being of known integrity and ability,) how to frame somewhat that might give us settlement, and they did so; and that I was not privy to their counsels, they know it.

When they had finished their model in some measure, or made a very good preparation of it, it [they] became communicative. They told me that except I would undertake the government, they thought things would hardly come to a composure and settlement, but blood and confusion would break in upon us. I denied it again and again, as God and those persons know, not complimentingly as they also know and as God knows.

I confess, after many arguments, and after the letting of me know that I did not receive anything that put me into any higher capacity than I was in before, but that it limited me and bound my hands to act nothing to the prejudice of the nations without consent of a Council until the Parliament [met], and then limited [me] by the Parliament as the Act of Government expresseth, I did accept it.

I might repeat this again to you, if it were needful, but I think I need not.

I was arbitrary in power, having the armies in the three nations under my command, and truly not very ill beloved by them, nor very ill beloved then by the people, by the good people. And I believe I should have been more beloved if they had known the truth, as things were before God, and in themselves, and before divers of these gentlemen whom I but now mentioned unto you.

I did, at the entreaty of divers persons of honour and quality, at the entreaty of very many of the chief officers of the army then present, and at their request, I did accept of the place and title of Protector, and was in the presence of the Commissioners of the Seal, the Judges, the Lord Mayor and Aldermen of the City of London, the soldiery, divers gentlemen, citizens, and divers other people and persons of quality, &c., accompanied to Westminster Hall, where I took my oath to this government. This was not done in a corner; it was open and public.

This government hath been exercised by a Council, with a desire to be faithful in all things, and amongst all other trusts to be faithful in calling this Parliament.

And thus I have given you a very bare and lean discourse, which truly I have been necessitated unto, and contracted in because of the unexpectedness of the occasion, and because I would not quite weary you nor myself. But this is a narrative that discovers to you the series of providence and of transactions leading me into this condition wherein I now stand.

* * *

I was a person who, from my first employment, was suddenly preferred and lifted up from lesser trusts to greater; from my first being a Captain of a Troop of Horse; and did labour as well as I could to discharge my trust; and God blessed me 'therein' as it pleased Him. And I did truly and plainly,—and in a way of foolish simplicity, as it was judged by very great and wise men, and good men too,—desire to make my instruments help me in that work. And I will deal plainly with you: I had a very worthy Friend then; and he was a very noble person, and I know his memory is very grateful to all,—Mr. John Hampden. At my first going out into this engagement, I saw our men were beaten at every hand. I did indeed; and desired him that he would make some additions to my Lord Essex's Army, of some new regiments; and I told him I would be serviceable to him in bringing such men in as I thought had a spirit that would do something in the work. This is very true that I tell you; God knows I lie not. "Your troops," said I, "are most of them old decayed serving-men, and tapsters, and such kind of fellows; and," said I, "their troops are gentlemen's sons, younger sons and persons of quality: do you think that the spirits of such base and mean fellows will ever be able to encounter gentlemen, that have honour and courage and resolution in them?" Truly I did represent to him in this manner conscientiously; and truly I did tell him: "You must get men of a spirit: and take it not ill what I say,—I know you will not,—of a spirit that is likely to go on as far as gentlemen will go:—or else you will be beaten still." I told him so; I did truly. He was a wise and worthy person; and he did think that I talked a good notion, but an impracticable one. . . . Truly I told him I could *do* somewhat in it. I did so,—'did this somewhat:' and truly I must needs say this to you, 'The result was,'—impute it to what you please,—I raised such men as had the fear of God before them, as made some conscience of what they did; and from that day forward, I must say to you, they were never beaten, and wherever they were engaged against the enemy, they beat continually. And truly this is matter of praise to God: —and it hath some instruction in it, To own men who are religious and godly. And so many of them as are peaceably and honestly and quietly disposed to live within 'rules of' Government, and will be subject to those Gospel rules of obeying Magistrates and living under Authority—I reckon no Godliness without that circle! Without that spirit, let it pretend what it will, it is diabolical, it is devilish, it is from diabolical spirits, from the depth of Satan's wickedness—Why truly I need not say more than to apply all this 'to the business we have in hand.'

I will be bold to apply this to our present purpose, because it is my all! I could say as all the world says, and run headily upon anything; but I must tender this 'my present answer' to you as a thing that sways upon my conscience; or else I were a knave and a deceiver. 'Well;' I tell you there are such men in this Nation; godly men of the same spirit,

men that will not be beaten down by a worldly or carnal spirit while they keep their integrity. And I deal plainly and faithfully with you, 'when I say:' I cannot think that God would bless an undertaking of anything, 'Kingship or whatever else,' which would, justly and with cause, grieve *them*. True, they may be troubled *without* cause;—and I must be a slave if I should comply with any such humour as that. But I say there are honest men and faithful men, true to the great things of the Government, namely the Liberty of the People, giving them what is due to them, and protecting this Interest (and I think verily God will bless you for what you have done in that)—But if I know, as indeed I do, that very generally good men do not swallow this Title,—though really it is no part of their goodness to be unwilling to submit to what a Parliament shall settle over them, yet I must say, it is my duty and my conscience to beg of you that there may be no hard things put upon me; things, I mean, hard to *them*, which they cannot swallow. . . .

I confess, for it behoves me to deal plainly with you—I must confess I would say—I hope I may not be misunderstood in this, for indeed I must be tender in what I say to such an audience:—I say I would have it understood, That in this argument I do not make a parallel between men of a different mind, 'mere dissentient individuals,' and a Parliament, 'as to,' Which shall have their desires. I know there is no comparison. Nor can it be urged upon me that my words have the least colour that way. For the Parliament seems to have given me liberty to say whatever is on my mind to you; as that 'indeed' is a tender of my humble reasons and judgment and opinion to *them:* and now if I think these objectors to the Kingship are such 'as I describe,' and 'that they' will be such; 'if I think' that they are faithful servants and will be so to the Supreme Authority, and the Legislative wheresoever it is,—if, I say, I should not tell you, knowing their minds to be so, then I should not be faithful. I am bound to tell you, to the end you may report it to the Parliament.

I will now say something for *myself*. As for my own mind, I do profess it, I am not a man scrupulous about words, or names, or such things. I have not 'hitherto clear direction'—but as I have the Word of God, and I hope shall ever have, for the rule of my conscience, for my information and direction; so, truly, if men have been led into dark paths through the providence and dispensations of God—why surely it is not to be objected to a man! For who can *love* to walk in the dark? But Providence doth often so dispose. And though a man may impute his own folly and blindness to Providence *sinfully*,—yet this must be at a man's own peril. The case may *be* that it is the Providence of God that doth lead men in darkness! I must needs say, I have had a great deal of experience of Providence; and though such experience is no rule without or against the Word, yet it is a very good expositor of the Word in many cases.

Truly the Providence of God hath laid aside this Title of King providentially *de facto:* and that not by sudden humour or passion; but it hath been by issue of as great deliberation as ever was in a Nation. It hath been by issue of Ten or Twelve Years Civil War, wherein much blood hath been shed. I will not dispute the justice of it when it was done; nor need I tell you what my opinion is in the case were it *de novo* to be done.

But if it be at all disputable; and a man comes and finds that God in His severity hath not only eradicated a whole Family, and thrust them out of the land, for reasons best known to Himself, but also hath made the issue and close of that to be the very eradication of a Name or Title—! Which *de facto* is 'the case.' It was not done by me, nor by them that tendered me the Government I now act in: it was done by the Long Parliament,—that was it. And God hath seemed Providential, 'seemed to appear as a Providence,' not only in striking at the Family but at the Name. And, as I said before, it is blotted out: it is a thing cast out by an Act of Parliament; it hath been kept out to this day. And as Jude saith, in another case, speaking of abominable sins that should be in the Latter Times,—he doth farther say, when he comes to exhort the Saints, he tells them, —they should "hate even the *garments* spotted with the flesh."

I beseech you think not that I bring this as an argument to prove anything. God hath seemed so to deal with the Persons and the Family that He blasted the very Title. And you know when a man comes, *a parte post,* to reflect, and see this *done,* this Title laid in the dust,—I confess I can come to no other conclusion. The like of this may make a strong impression upon such weak men as I am;—and perhaps upon weaker men (if there be any such) it will make a stronger. I will not seek to set up that which Providence hath destroyed and laid in the dust; I would not build Jericho again! And this is somewhat to me, and to my judgment and my conscience. This, in truth, it is that that hath an awe upon my spirit.

ROBERT S. PAUL (1918–   ) is a Professor of Church History at Pittsburgh Theological Seminary in Pennsylvania. After training at Oxford, he served in an English pastorate and with the Ecumenical Institute in Switzerland before moving to the United States. Paul's interests focus on the role of Christianity in Western development, on the ecumenical movement, and on preparing the church to understand its proper role in its total environment. His studies have alternated between pastoral and historical theology and seventeenth century history. Paul's life of Cromwell is his major work and has absorbed him for over a decade. As one might expect, the biography offers religious dimensions unavailable elsewhere.*

Robert S. Paul

The Christian in Politics

Like some great symbolic statue the figure of Oliver Cromwell stands at the mouth of a harbour in world history. Beyond him is a new world—a world of new discoveries in science and politics, a world where the old laws and honoured conventions are superseded, and where new freedoms and perhaps new cynicisms have taken their place. But although he stands at the gateway to modern history, and although he and the Revolution he personified are symbolic of our expanding outlook and new-born liberties, his face is towards the civilizations of the past, and he is firmly set within the great expanse of faith that will ever divide the old world from the new.

That is where this book begins and ends —with the contention that to understand a man who lived in an age of faith, we must treat seriously the faith of his age. Modern research has presented us with a wealth of facts about the seventeenth century quite unknown to Mark Noble living a bare hundred years after the Lord Protector's death; modern methods of literary criticism have made it possible to get to the actual words that were written and spoken in a way which was impossible even to the inspiration of Thomas Carlyle; modern conventions of historical objectivity enable us to break through three hundred years of prejudiced writings by Tories who hated Cromwell for killing Charles Stuart, and Whigs who hated him for destroying the monarchy;

*From Robert S. Paul, *The Lord Protector* (London, 1955) pp. 381–393. Used by permission from the author and the publishers: Lutterworth Press, London, E.C. 4; and Wm. B. Eerdmans Co., Grand Rapids, Michigan.

33

but with all these advantages we shall be immeasurably the poorer if we underestimate or ignore the religion which gave Cromwell the incentive to do the things he did, and to be the man he was. . . . Far more must go into the interpretation of historical character than the systematic collation of material facts, however comprehensively presented or accurately assessed; and in this "the spirit of the age" is an all-important piece of historical evidence which must not be ignored. . . .

As we have seen earlier, there was a widely-held historical convention behind the systematic blackening of Cromwell's character, and it is significant that in damning him his enemies could not hide their respect for his qualities. Republicans like Edmund Ludlow found least to commend in him, for to them the Lord Protector was the Great Apostate who had sinned against the light, but Lucy Hutchinson, who was not behind Ludlow in detestation of the Protectorate, compared Cromwell's ambition very favourably with that of Lambert—"the one was gallant and great, the other had nothing but an unworthy pride." Oliver's personal courage and magnanimity, she said, "upheld him against all enemies and malcontents."

All these were among his critics and opponents, yet however much they defame his ambition from their several points of view, they do not deny—and the hint is even in Ludlow—his ability to govern well. This is illustrated not only in the sincere admiration which his foreign policy won from royalists like Edward Hyde and Dr. Bates, but also in their grudging recognition of the law and order that he achieved at home. They both remark upon the impartiality with which the Law was dispensed during the Protectorate in all cases where the security of the regime

was not threatened, and Bates says that as a result of Oliver's administration "trade began to prosper; and in a word, gentle Peace to flourish all over England."

A further characteristic of his government, noted by friend and foe alike, was what Lucy Hutchinson calls his "magnanimity." There was a sympathy and concern for human suffering in Oliver Cromwell which appears to have shown itself to everyone but the Catholic Irish, and this trait is the more remarkable when we consider the age in which he lived, and the military and political arts in which he became adept. However, it was evident not only in personal relationship with those who had some claim upon his sympathy, but also towards many of his enemies. Mrs. Hutchinson described a plot against his life by Colonel Rich and the Commissaries Watson and Staines, and says that having proved their testimony before the Council of State to be false, Oliver straightway spoke up in their defence before the Council. We have seen previously that one who knew him very well described him as "naturally compassionate towards objects in distresse;" but it was Clarendon, the Secretary of State to Charles II's exiled court, who gave the most striking testimony to the Protector's clemency:

He was not a man of blood, and totally declined Machiavel's method, which prescribes, upon any alteration of a government, as a thing absolutely necessary, to cut off all the heads of those, and extirpate their families, who are friends to the old [one]. And it was confidently reported, that in the council of officers it was more than once proposed that there might be a general massacre of all the royal party, as the only expedient to secure the government; but Cromwell would never consent to it.

The Protector's government took its temper from the Protector's character, and when we are able to get behind the jumble of eulogy and calumny, the character which is presented to us by Oliver's own contemporaries is that of a man of outstanding ability, of justice and impartiality in anything which did not jeopardize his rule, and of remarkable clemency to many of his enemies.

Yet to leave the description of his character without mentioning his religion would be to present the body without a soul. Oliver said of himself, "No man, no man, but a man mistaken and greatly mistaken, could think that I, that hath a burden upon my back for the space of fifteen or sixteen years—unless he would beforehand judge me an atheist—would seek such a place as I bear." And that is the issue: Cromwell's religion was either central within his life, or else he was a cynical unbeliever. No judicious historian could deny that within the Lord Protector's career, often hidden to himself, material considerations, dissembled motives and lesser ends played their part; yet all through his life there is the consistent evidence of sincere personal religion and the influence of his theological and ecclesiastical concepts is too evident to be disregarded or explained away as merely the thought-forms of his day. They were the thought-forms of his day, but there was all Heaven and Hell behind them.

In 1656 the Venetian ambassador wrote of the Protector, "It cannot be denied that by his ability and industry he has contributed to his own greatness," but he added, "with all his abounding courage, good sense and natural prudence, all these qualities would have served him for nothing if circumstances had not opened the way to greatness." The Italian envoy perhaps would not have appreciated the religious significance of his own

words, but it was in the amazing circumstances of his own career that Cromwell discerned and tested the validity of the divine call that he believed was his. That strict doctrine of Providence which held with John Calvin that "the righteous are the special objects of His favour, the wicked and profane the special objects of His severity" was not only the stimulus of Cromwell's single-minded purpose throughout the civil wars, and the foundation of his claim to a vocation of statesmanship, but during the vicissitudes of the Protectorate it was also the one sure anchor of hope that God would be with him to the end. It is possible to criticize this interpretation of Providence, or the exclusive view of "Election" and "Grace" in Calvinism, or the literal Biblicism and extravagant apocalyptic hopes of Puritanism, but however much these ideas may be criticized, they were factors, and often governing factors, in conditioning the life and thought of seventeenth century England, and we disregard them only at the expense of misinterpreting the period.

In the same way it is possible to ridicule the idea of a troop of cavalry or Council of Army officers organized as a "gathered Church," but it was recognized by Richard Baxter after Naseby, and that keen critic admitted the honesty of Cromwell's intention when he said, "I conjecture, that at his first choosing such men into his Troop, it was the very Esteem and Love of Religious men that principally moved him." Sir Ernest Barker has commented that "The habit of the Independents was always a habit of congregationalism. Even the Independent army debated, because it was a congregation as well as an army." In Baxter's testimony, in the nature of the Army Council and its discussions, and in the continuous influence of the Army's opinion on Cromwell's own decisions, we see that these words were true not only in a general sense, but also in the particular and personal sense of a man's relationship with his "Church."

It is within this kind of setting that Oliver Cromwell saw his own divinely appointed task on behalf of the people of England—or perhaps more accurately, on behalf of the "godly" people of England. He was only accidentally—or "providentially"—a soldier and a statesman, and he owned few political theories that could be regarded as inviolable. It was "lawfull to passe through any formes of Government for the accomplishing of his ends," and he reminded the Army officers in 1647 that the Hebrews had experimented with several different kinds of government. "If you should change the government to the best of it," he commented, "it is but, as Paul says, 'dross and dung in comparison of Christ':" forms of government, no less than individuals, were to be brought under the judgment of the Biblical revelation, and the proof of divine approval was to be sought in that "chain of Providence" by which nations and individuals are led.

It might be thought at first that because Cromwell's sense of vocation was based upon personal experience it therefore must have been entirely subjective—an arbitrary declaration of his own purpose that brooked no argument or interference: "Come, come, I will put an end to your prating . . . call them in, call them in!" A closer study, however, will show that his sense of vocation is not to be dismissed so summarily, for it was endorsed not only by the actual success of his undertakings, but it was also tested by the Word of Scripture. The importance of these factors can be seen when Cromwell's career is compared with more modern dictators, for whereas his conception of duty might lead him to act dictatorially, it could never lead him to act amorally, much less contrary to Biblical morality in so far as he understood it: Cromwell might misinterpret the Biblical standards, he might be guilty of faulty exegesis, but he could never deliberately mishandle Scripture, for he had placed himself under the judgment of its revelation. Similarly with regard to the doctrine of Providence, he could not believe that God was with him, unless he could assure himself of a clean conscience; for, according to his own beliefs, his success was entirely due to the singleness of purpose with which he and his troops had tried to obey God's will. There may be occasions when we are able to discern beneath Oliver's passionate assertions of high calling the shape of less worthy motives, but he never gives any indication in private letter or public utterance that these motives were consciously recognized by him: Cromwell acted like a prophet, and the true prophet "is one who can say with Paul, 'I was not disobedient to the heavenly vision'."

Throughout his public life we see the future Lord Protector struggling to reconcile these fundamental convictions first with the military and political needs of the nation, secondly with his own responsibility within the nation, and finally with the position of the English Protectorate within the context of world affairs. Perhaps the way in which he met the circumstances of his time on the basis of his professed beliefs tells us more about his character than any summary of his personal attributes.

At this stage we must point out that our study has a relevance to certain theological problems which are often regarded as belonging exclusively to the present century. The continued interest in Cromwell is perhaps due in part to the enigma of character and in part to the unique place he occupied on the threshold of this world of utilitarian science and political pragmatism. He brings theology and politics to a single focus: we think we understand the meaning of his actions only too well, but we are slightly shocked to hear him describe his motives in a language which we have long since forgotten. Perhaps, however, it is in the fact that Cromwell continued to use that language in a society which was beginning to demonstrate many features common to our own, that he continues to be a significant figure with something to say to us.

If — as I would agree — "all political problems are at bottom theological," then the rude entry of the totalitarian State into western Christendom demands that Christian theologians must re-think the relationship between religion and politics generally, and the theological foundations of the State in particular. It is one of the strange tricks of history that at the time when so many modern questions made their first appearance those who were responsible for government in Britain and America were the spiritual sons of English Puritanism. Fresh from the exclusiveness of the "gathered" churches, and from a separation from the muddy world of affairs which was imposed as much by their beliefs as by exile and proscription, they suddenly found themselves responsible for government in important States. They discovered that they could not avoid participation in secular society and the problems it brought with it, but they had to face these problems without preconceived theories and solely upon the principles of their Biblical faith. For this reason the career of Cromwell forces us to consider seriously the place of the

State in Christian theology, and challenges us to define the limitations of politics as a "Christian" vocation.

It also makes us question again our understanding of Providence in history, and the significance of the chain of special circumstances that makes us what we are, in shaping our own personal vocation under God. Baxter said that Cromwell and his men

thought that God had called them by Successes to Govern and take care of the Commonwealth, and of the Interest of his People in the Land; and that if they stood by and suffered the Parliament to do that which they thought was dangerous, it would be required at their hands, whom they thought God had made Guardians of the Land.

Stated in its crudest form this interpretation of the relationship between Providence and Vocation will be rejected, but we cannot escape the issues which the career of Oliver and his men raised. Is there any inner necessity in the events of Providence which determines the ultimate victory of "Good?" and if so, what relationship does this bear to our individual histories? When Dr. Reinhold Niebuhr says that the Christian "takes the historic struggle for justice and freedom seriously and knows that God will not negate what is good in history," that was precisely Cromwell's contention; but he believed that to be as true for individuals as it was within the pattern of world history — with this safeguard, that God's Providence would vindicate his personal vocation only in so far as he could meet it with a clear conscience and an absolute integrity.

In the same way Cromwell's life raises the question of Christian standards of conduct within a secular society, about which Protestantism has had singularly little to say. Dr. J. C. Bennett has shown that the answers of Protestant Christianity are extremely complex, and do not avoid the ultimate responsibility of decision by the individual Christian: "the burden upon the mind and the conscience of the individual Christian is very great for he must finally bring together all of these factors that have been outlined and make his own decision. For the Protestant there is no escape from this burden." It would appear to be quite unscriptural to avoid moral decisions of this kind, but it is one thing to leave the individual Christian free to accept his rightful responsibility, and another thing to leave him so bereft of guidance that he is unable to make his decisions in a Christian and responsible manner. For this reason the wrestlings of Cromwell and his colleagues are of direct relevance to our contemporary understanding of "the Christian in Society." Their answer to the problem was what we have called the "dual ethic."

Again, in its crudest form the theology is obviously unacceptable, but the modification of the principle was just as significant as the principle itself, and in at least two ways the solution put forward by Cromwell and his contemporaries deserves careful consideration by those who are concerned with the problems of moral theology today. First, in the recognition of Justice as the norm of public action and the aim of civil society, they seem to have recognized a principle which only recently has been taken seriously by theologians. Secondly, from hints in the speeches of Cromwell, Ireton and others we have seen that they conceived this not as a Hebrew standard, but as Christian. The Old Testament ethic was to be applied only "according to the mind of Christ:" Justice was to be the goal of the State, but love was to be the motive of the Christian statesman, or, to see the same idea from a slightly different angle,

the State was to seek Justice as its highest good, but it was to be Justice upheld by Mercy, and Law interpreted by Love.

To pass from the theoretical to the practical, perhaps of all the Protector's experiments, the one which would most repay careful study is his settlement of religion. Since 1660 it has never received the attention it deserved, no doubt partly because it had had such a short time in which to justify itself—a matter of five or six years—and partly because it had been brought into being by a discredited government.

By the *Instrument of Government* and the *Humble Petition and Advice*, "the Christian religion as contained in the Scriptures" was established as the officially recognized religion of the three nations of Britain. A Profession of Faith was compiled, and all ministers who agreed with this statement, although differing in matters of worship and discipline, were to be "fit and capable . . . of any trust, promotion or employment whatsoever in these nations." By this means the Protector established not a particular Church with its individual orders and theory of Church government, but the Christian Protestant religion; for the first time in history the State had established an ecclesiastical system in which more than one form of churchmanship was recognized and was able to take its full part. What this could teach us within the sphere of church relationships in England, or within the Ecumenical Movement at large, only serious study can reveal; but it certainly issues a challenge. The present system of Establishment in England, which recognizes one Church in nominal control of a country that it is increasingly impotent to evangelize, is an anomaly which is tolerated only because we are afraid that its injudicious exit would open the door to a completely secular State; but the time has surely come when the needs of society demand that the conventional basis of national religion should be broadened, so that the responsibilities of pastoral care and of evangelism can be shared.

In the same way, the Cromwellian settlement of religion was a practical experiment in a federal conception of the Catholic Church which as Canon J. E. Fison has suggested may very well be the way ahead in ecumenical relationships. At the heart of the system there was a Congregational—or rather, Biblical—conception of Covenant: just as the individual members were within the Covenant of Grace, so they and their churches recognized that they were in covenant relationship with each other. It was a system which depended for its smooth working upon this mutual recognition of membership in the Body of Christ, and the few years it was allowed were at least sufficient to show that where such recognition exists, the unity of the Church can be made evident by other means than immediate organic union. Whether Episcopacy would ever have found its way into the system, we shall never know, but on the face of it there was no practical reason why it should not have done so, once its political associations had been forgotten, and as soon as it was ready to accept a covenant relationship with others.

Cromwell became a "dictator," but it was not from choice. Events had their own way of pushing him to the fore and ultimately to the head of affairs, and the very circumstances of his rise prevented that popular recognition which would have set the seal to his mission. Nevertheless, although only a person "mistaken and greatly mistaken" would imagine that he consciously schemed for the position which he came to occupy, when the chance of taking the government presented itself he took it firmly. It is within that paradox that what he did sometimes seems to belie what he said.

Yet to suggest a fundamental hypocrisy —whether on the grounds advanced by seventeenth century royalists, or on those put forward by twentieth century realists —is to offer a solution too simple to be acceptable. It is too simple because it ignores what is perhaps the most singular fact of Cromwell's career—that throughout the vast accumulation of his uttered thought that has come down to us, never once does he admit a lesser motive in private conversation, public speech, or in his most intimate correspondence. No man could have forwarded his own self-interest to achieve a public career of such magnitude without giving some hints of his ambition in word or letter, if personal ambition were the only or even the predominant motive of the career; and yet few men in history appear to have acted more consistently and with a clearer conscience than Oliver Cromwell. The explanation of this can only be that within Cromwell's own mind his ambition was itself the instrument of a greater cause which he served with absolute sincerity.

When we have given due weight to the motives of self-interest and preservation, and when we have faced the fact that the Independents had either to rule or pay the penalty for their rebellion, there remains a paradox within Cromwell's career which has a religious cause; for although religion was not the original occasion for the outbreak of civil war, "God brought it to that issue at last," Oliver said, "and gave it unto us by way of redundancy, and at last it proved to be that which was most dear to us." To Oliver himself the issue of religion had become central, and it was simply the issue of winning liberty for "all species of Protestants, to worship God according to their own light and consciences," but the paradox is in the fact that this liberty could be guaranteed in no other way but by his own personal rule: Episcopalian King, Presbyterian Parliament, Sectarian Convention—they all gave ample evidence of the "strange itch" of persecution that Cromwell feared and detested. He had to rule, or else be prepared to see the religious freedom that he prized above all other earthly benefits disappear either into the prison of uniformity or into a madhouse of anarchy. It was the major tragedy of his rule that in defending one liberty he seemed to threaten all the rest, that in standing as the champion of freedom he often appeared as the epitome of tyranny.

Nevertheless we must ask ourselves whether at that time religious liberty could have been won in any other way. Amid the political dangers of our own day, if this essential freedom should again be put in jeopardy, who could say now how it could best be defended, or what forms of government would be justifiable in its defence? Perhaps a good dictatorship must always be bad government but Oliver Cromwell believed that both spiritual coercion and political anarchy were infinitely worse. It was for this reason that his deepest convictions and his own advancement became identified, and the Lord's "unprofitable servant" accepted the call to become his country's Lord Protector.

The French Huguenot and distinguished historian MERLE D'AUBIGNÉ (1796–1872) was in most respects an orthodox Presbyterian. He wanted, however, to see church and state dissociated and would never condemn episcopacy, on the one hand, or denigrate congregationalism, on the other. This tolerance and breadth of view put him in sympathy with Cromwell. Moreover, his extensive researches into the history of the Reformation helped him place Cromwell in a broad historical perspective, one that differs from that of R. S. Paul.*

J. H. Merle D'Aubigné

Defender of Protestantism

Cromwell was sincere, he was true: this is the first but not the only point we shall undertake to establish.

Protestantism was on its trial. There can be no doubt that the principles of civil liberty, which the family of James the First desired to crush, but which eventually triumphed in the English nation, and which have raised it to such an elevation, had a great share in this struggle; and no one man did more than Oliver towards their development. But the principal thing which drew down the anger of his enemies was Protestantism, in its boldest not less than it clearest form; and the false imputation borne by this eminent man was essentially the work of Popery. In the seventeenth century, when the Protestant princes were everywhere in-timidated, weakened and dumb, and when some of them were making ready for a fatal apostasy, Cromwell was the only one to declare himself in the face of all Europe the protector of the true faith. He even induced Cardinal Mazarin, a prince of the Romish Church, to connive at his generous designs. This is a crime for which he has never been pardoned, and for which his enemies have inflicted a scandalous revenge. In this task so much perseverance and skill have been employed, that not only enlightened Catholics, but even Protestants themselves have been deceived. We feel no inclination to adopt the hatred and calumnies of Rome, and we sympathize with Protestantism wherever it is to be found. This will not lead us to extenuate the faults of those

* From J. H. Merle D'Aubigné, *The Protector: A Vindication* (Edinburgh, 1848) pp. 26–34 and 405–425.

who have been its supporters; nor will their defects blind us against their good qualities. In the struggle between Protestantism and Popery, which took place in the British Isles in Cromwell's time, the noblest part indisputably belongs to the former; and the mistakes of its adherents are unimportant compared with the excessive immorality and the frightful cruelties of which the friends of Rome were guilty. . . . Cromwell, during the season of his power, was really the *Protector* of European, and, in particular, of French Protestantism. As I am myself descended from Huguenot refugees, it seemed to me that I had a debt to pay to this illustrious man. There were, perhaps, some of my forefathers among those inhabitants of Nismes, whom the powerful intervention of the English chief rescued from the vengeance of the soldiers of Louis XIV., already marching against that city to execute the orders of the court to the last extremity. "Nobody can wonder," said Clarendon, a man who, it is well known, had no great love for the Protector, and who wrote shortly after the event, "that Cromwell's memory still remains in those parts and with those people in great veneration." Even King James was struck with the esteem which the French Protestants in general entertained towards Oliver.

The vindication, or rather the restoration, of the Protector's memory, has already begun; and perhaps no one can do more for it than Mr. Carlyle has accomplished. I think, however, that there is room for some improvement. Oliver has been presented as a hero to the world; I present him as a Christian to Christians — to Protestant Christians. . . .

It is seldom that a great man is a Christian, but Cromwell was both. The result has been, that men of the world have scouted him as a hypocrite. . . . It would be an act of great meanness, a criminal falsehood, if those who, by studying the life of this great man, find in him an upright heart and a sincere piety, should unite their voices with those of his detractors. We, on our part, desire to the utmost of our ability to renounce all participation in this gross imposture. We shall say with Dryden, in the last verse of his stanzas on the Death of Cromwell:

His ashes in a peaceful urn shall rest;
  His name a great example stands to show
How strangely high endeavours may be blest,
  Where piety and valour jointly go.

What most distinguishes Cromwell above all great men, and especially above all statesmen, is the predominance in him of the evangelical and Christian element. . . .

Christian element existed not only in Oliver's person; but also in his government. We may contemplate in him the true union between Church and State; namely, the love and the wisdom of God in the hearts of the rulers. Cromwell thought that the political and national greatness of Britain could not be established in a firm manner, unless the pure Gospel was communicated to the people, and unless a truly christian life flowed through the veins of the nation. Its blood was frozen; and he thought that in order to restore their former vigour to the British people, Christianity must again set their hearts beating. Of all political systems, surely this is as good as any other.

The Reformation and the Romish heirarchy, Oliver and the Pope, both thought that the influence of the Church was necessary to the prosperity of the State. But although they agreed on the *necessity* of this influence, they differed wholly as to its *nature*.

In Oliver's system the influence of the Church upon the State is purely internal

—it is moral or religious; while in the papal system this influence is essentially external, being ecclesiastical or political. For Cromwell, the Church was the invisible Church with its spiritual powers; for the Pope, it was the visible hierarchy of Rome with its plots and intrigues.

Humanity ought to be sanctified and glorified: this is the function of Christianity. But, according to Oliver and Protestantism, this great object will be obtained by the conversion of every individual man. Faith brings to man a new life, purifies all his natural capacities, and consecrates them to God. Undoubtedly the Church is the means by which this work of restoration is accomplished. But it is not by its outward organization, by its clerical framework, by magical virtues concealed in the sacraments, that it is effected; it is brought about by the preaching of the Word, and by the operation of the Holy Ghost.

To advance this work of regeneration is not exclusively the province of the ministers of the Church; it belongs to all Christians. . . . Oliver insisted on this point in Scotland. Christ dwells in every believer, and He cannot abide there in inactivity. If in heaven He is, for the salvation of His people, prophet, priest and king; on earth they should imitate Him, and be, for His glory, prophets, priests, and kings.

Life and activity—a life and an activity conformable to the law of God—being thus carried by evangelical Christianity into each individual, are also carried into the mass, into society, into the Church, and into the State. In those nations where the evangelical spirit prevails, the moral, religious, and intellectual life will be developed; every force will be set in motion; liberty on the one hand, submission to the laws on the other, will be blessings permanently acquired; and the nation will arrive at a degree of power, greatness, and glory, that others will never attain.

Although in the bosom of Protestant nations evangelical Christianity is far from having reached the perfection it ought to possess, it is sufficient to compare these nations with others, in order to perceive that such is, in general, the effect of those principles of which Oliver was one of the most eminent advocates. In Great Britain and Spain we have a signal illustration of this truth.

If Cromwell salutes the English nation, as "a very great people,—the best people in the world,"—it is because they are "a people that have the highest and clearest profession among them of the greatest glory, namely Religion." If some who desire to have "horse-races, cock-fightings, and the like," say, "They in France are so and so!" Oliver replies: "Have they *the Gospel* as we have? They have seen the sun but a little. We have great lights!" . . . He declares what has been the principal means employed by him to effect the good of the British nation: "I have been seeking of God—from the great God—a blessing upon you (the paraliament), and upon these nations." In his closet, alone, and on his knees, he wrestled with God to promote the good of his people, to whose political interests one cause with him was superior to all others—the cause of Christ; and Cromwell knew that it was only by being faithful to this, that he could secure the true interests of his nation. . . .

Nothing was more offensive to Oliver than to hear it said that it was *his* wisdom and *his* skill which had given liberty, dominion, and glory to his people. He tore off the wreath that some would thus have placed around his brows, and like those mysterious beings in the apocalypse, he cast his crown before the throne of the Lamb, saying: *"Thou* art worthy,

O Lord, to receive glory, and honour, and power!".. .

When Oliver set forth religion as the true source of a nation's prosperity, it was not a religion of impressions only, an enthusiastic and fanatical religion; no! It was a moral religion. In his eyes, morality was quite as important as doctrine: he knew that *faith without works is dead.* "I did hint to you my thoughts about the reformation of manners," he said to parliament on the 17th of September 1656. "And those abuses that are in this nation through disorder, are a thing which should be much in your hearts. It is that which, I am confident, is a description and character of the interest you have been engaged against, the cavalier interest: the badge and character of countenancing profaneness, disorder, and wickedness in all places—and whatever is most of kin to these, and most agrees with what is Popery, and with the profane nobility and gentry of this nation! . . . If it lives in us, therefore; I say, if it be in the general heart of the nation, it is a thing I am confident our liberty and prosperity depend upon—Reformation. Make it a shame to see men bold in sin and profaneness, and God will bless you. . . .

Oliver exerted all his eloquence to persuade the Parliament that piety and decision in God's cause could alone save England and Protestantism. There was never, perhaps, a man more decided than Cromwell, and he would fain have imparted some of this spirit to all who had the means of influencing the prosperity of Great Britian ·and of the Protestant world. . . .

Such, then, was Oliver's policy: "Be united in faith and love to Christ! Suppress everything that is evil, and encourage whatsoever is of godliness."

This is not the policy of the Pope. The kingdom of God, says he, is in the Church; the Church is in the hierarchy; and the hierarchy is in the Pope. The Church finds the State far from God, without life from above; and imparts to it that life, not by regenerating the individuals who compose that society, but by attaching them in a mass to its own ecclesiastical organization. If the State submits to the Church, it is a Christian state; if it opposes the Church, that is, the pope, it is not of Christ or of His covenant. Popery does not positively exclude the internal work, which is the essence of Protestantism; but no great importance is attached to it. All that Romanism requires is submission to the papacy, and an outward, legal morality. And how low the standard of that morality has been brought may be learned from the classbooks employed in her theological seminaries.

While the Protestant principle gives a nation liberty, life, and order; the Romanist principle, on the contrary, brings to it slavery, disorder, and death. . . .

This servitude, which Popery brings on the nations, necessarily leads in their case to a moral and intellectual torpor, which erelong becomes a political and industrial death.

Such is the system which Oliver Cromwell rejected, and for which he substituted the Gospel.

He was wrong when he determined to forbid the mass; and we have seen that afterwards he was willing to tolerate it. Full liberty of conscience to all was his great principle, and it will gradually become the device of the whole world. But that was not properly the question, which was political rather than religious. It was this: Could the subjects of a foreign prince be active citizens in another state, and take part in its administration? . . .

For him there was, however, another element in this question. The prince of the Vatican was in his eyes a malignant power, the *man of sin,* who necessarily brings desolation and destruction upon the nations. . . .

Much has been said of Cromwell's ambition. *This* made him take up arms, *this* made him become Protector, *this* agitated him during the discussion on the kingship! The ambition of one man! . . . and is this all that men can see in his life? It is a paltry manner of viewing history. In truth it was a very different thing and very different thoughts which filled Oliver's bosom. It was not *a feather in his cap* that occupied his mind: he was fighting the great battle against the papacy and royalty of the Middle Ages—the greatest that history has had to describe since the establishment of Christianity and the struggle of the Reformation.

The result of this battle was the deliverance of the present age and of ages yet to come. Without Cromwell, humanly speaking, liberty would have been lost not only to England, but to Europe. Even Hume in one place ascribes this immense and glorious result to the puritans. We must add, that the defeat of liberty would have been the defeat of the Gospel.

In the seventeenth century there were but two men: Louis XIV and Oliver Cromwell; the former representing absolutism and Roman Catholicism; the latter, evangelical Christianity and liberty. . . . Between them—between their systems, if not between their persons— the struggle was fought; and the victory, although slow and long disputed, particularly in France, remained with Oliver. They are the representatives of two principles—of two worlds. These two gigantic figures are each raised on a lofty pedestal; and their shadows fall not only on their own age, but extend over all future times. . . .

God works by instruments; and if there is any one man who, in times past, has contributed more than another, more than all others, to the wonders of the present day, that man is . . . Oliver Cromwell. The existing greatness of England is but the realization of the plan he had conceived.

A Scot who began to shed his strict Calvinist upbringing during university days at Edinburgh, THOMAS CARLYLE (1795–1881) became a literary giant and a renowned historical biographer after a long struggle with poverty. As the first editor of Cromwell's extant *Letters and Speeches,* he not only performed an invaluable service by allowing Cromwell to speak for himself but also presented a striking and original view of Cromwell in his commentary. For Carlyle, history was the sum of the biographies of great men. Their success was justification enough for their policies, and the blind masses needed heroic guidance. His numerous biographical pieces, short and long, included studies of Frederick the Great and Schiller as well as Oliver Cromwell. Scorning democracy, ballot-boxes, parliaments, and sentimental humanitarianism he was neither without human sympathy nor a proto-Nazi. Vivid, imaginative, fervid, and vehement, his style and his point of view are without likeness in English literature.*

Thomas Carlyle

The Hero Cometh

Letters and authentic Utterances of Oliver lie scattered, in print and manuscript in a hundred repositories, in all varieties of condition and environment. Most of them, all the important of them, have already long since been printed and again printed; but we cannot in general say, ever read; too often it is apparent that the very editor of these poor utterances had, if reading mean understanding, never *read* them. They stand in their old spelling; mispunctuated, misprinted, unelucidated, unintelligible, defaced with the dark incrustations too well known to students of that Period. The Speeches above all, as hitherto set forth in *The Somers Tracts,* in *The Milton State Papers,* in *Burton's Diary,* and other such Books, excel human belief; certainly no such agglomerate of opaque confusions, printed and reprinted; of darkness on the back of darkness, thick and threefold; is known to me elsewhere in the history of things spoken or printed by human creatures. Of these Speeches, all except one, which was published by authority at the time, I have to believe myself, not very exultingly, to be the first actual reader for nearly two centuries past.

Nevertheless these Documents do exist,

*From Thomas Carlyle, *Oliver Cromwell's Letters and Speeches* (London, 1846) pp. 60–66; also from *On Heroes, Hero Worship, and the Heroic in History* (London, 1889) pp. 196–203. The concluding paragraph of this extract is from *The Letters & Speeches,* p. 777.

authentic though defaced; and invite every one who would know that Period, to study them till they become intelligible again. The words of Oliver Cromwell— the meaning *they* had, must be worth recovering in that point of view. To collect these Letters and authentic Utterances, as one's reading yielded them, was a comparatively grateful labour; to correct them, elucidate and make them legible again, was a good historical study. Surely "a wise memory" would wish to preserve among men the written and spoken words of such a man—and as for the "wise oblivion," that is already, by Time and Accident, done to our hand. Enough is already lost and destroyed; we need not, in this particular case, omit farther.

Accordingly, whatever words authentically proceeding from Oliver himself I could anywhere find yet surviving, I have here gathered; and will now, with such minimum of annotation as may suit that object, offer them to the reader. That is the purport of the Book. I have ventured to believe that, to certain patient earnest readers, these old dim Letters of a noble English Man might, as they had done to myself, become dimly legible again; might dimly present, better than all other evidence, the noble figure of the Man himself again. Certainly there is Historical instruction in these Letters:— Historical, and perhaps other and better. At least, it is with Heroes and god-inspired men that I, for my part, would far rather converse, in what dialect soever they speak! Great, ever fruitful; profitable for reproof, for encouragement, for building up in manful purposes and works, are the words of those that in their day were men. I will advise serious persons, interested in England past or present, to try if they can read a little in these Letters of Oliver Cromwell, a man once deeply interested in the same object.

Heavy as it is, and dim and obsolete, there may be worse reading, for such persons in our time.

For the rest, if each Letter look dim, and have little light, after all study;— yet let the Historical reader reflect, such light as it has cannot be disputed at all. These words, expository of that day and hour, Oliver Cromwell did see fittest to be written down. The Letter hangs there in the dark abysses of the Past; if like a star almost extinct, yet like a real star; fixed; about which there is no cavilling possible. That autograph Letter, it was once all luminous as a burning beacon, every word of it a live coal, in its time; it was once a piece of the general fire and light of Human Life, that Letter! Neither is it yet entirely extinct; well read, there is still in it light enough to exhibit its own *self;* nay to diffuse a faint authentic twilight some distance round it. Heaped embers which in the daylight looked black, may still look *red* in the utter darkness. These Letters of Oliver will convince any man that the past did exist! By degrees the combined small twilights may produce a kind of general feeble twilight, rendering the Past credible, the Ghosts of the Past in some glimpses of them visible! Such is the effect of contemporary letters always; and I can very confidently recommend Oliver's as good of their kind. A man intent on forcing for himself some path through that gloomy chaos called History of the Seventeenth Century, and looking face to face upon the same, may perhaps try it by this method as hopefully as by another. Here is an irregular row of beacon fires, once all luminous as suns; and with a certain inextinguishable erubescence still, in the abysses of the dead deep Night. Let us look here. In shadowy outlines, in dimmer and dimmer crowding forms, the very figure of the old dead Time itself may perhaps be faintly discernible here!

I called these Letters good—but withal only good of their kind. No eloquence, elegance, not always even clearness of expression, is to be looked for in them. They are written with far other than literary aims; written, most of them, in the very flame and conflagration of a revolutionary struggle, and with an eye to the despatch of indispensable pressing business alone; but it will be found, I conceive, that for such end they are well written. Superfluity, as if by a natural law of the case, the writer has had to discard; whatsoever quality *can* be dispensed with is indifferent to him. With unwieldy movement, yet with a great solid step he presses through, towards his object; has marked out very decisively what the real steps towards it are; discriminating well the essential from the extraneous;—forming to himself, in short, a true, not an untrue picture of the business that is to be done. There is in these Letters as I have said above, a *silence* still more significant of Oliver to us than any speech they have. Dimly we discover features of an Intelligence, and Soul of a Man, greater than any speech. The Intelligence that can, with full satisfaction to itself, come out in eloquent speaking, in musical singing, is, after all, a small Intelligence. He that works and *does* some Poem, not he that merely *says* one, is worthy of the name of Poet. Cromwell, emblem of the dumb English, is interesting to me by the very inadequacy of his speech. Heroic insight, valour and belief, without words—how noble is it in comparison to eloquent words without heroic insight! . . .

Surely it is far enough from probable that these Letters of Cromwell, written originally for quite other objects, and selected not by the Genius of History, but by blind Accident which has saved them hitherto and destroyed the rest—

can illuminate for a modern man this Period of our Annals, which for all moderns, we may say, has become a gulf of bottomless darkness! Not so easily will the modern man domesticate himself in a scene of things every way so foreign to him. Nor could any measurable exposition of mine, on this present occasion, do much to illuminate the dead dark world of the Seventeenth Century, into which the reader is about to enter. He will gradually get to understand, as I have said, that the Seventeenth Century did exist; that it was not a waste rubbish continent of Rushworth-Nalson State Papers, of Philosophical Scepticisms, Dilettantisms, Dryas-dust Torpedoisms;—but an actual flesh-and-blood Fact; with colour in its cheeks, with awful august heroic thoughts in its heart, and at last with steel sword in its hand! Theoretically this is a most small postulate, conceded at once by everybody; but practiacally it is a very large one, seldom or never conceded; the due practical conceding of it amounts to much, indeed to the sure promise of all. I will venture to give the reader two little pieces of advice, which, if his experience resemble mine, may prove furthersome to him in this inquiry; they include the essence of all that I have discovered respecting it.

The first is, By no means to credit the wide-spread report that these Seventeenth-Century Puritans were superstitious crackbrained persons; given up to enthusiasm, the most part of them; the minor ruling part being cunning men, who knew how to assume the dialect of the others, and thereby, as skilful Machiavels, to dupe them. This is a wide-spread report; but an untrue one. I advise my reader to try precisely the opposite hypothesis. To consider that his Fathers, who had thought about this World very seriously indeed, and with very considerable thinking faculty indeed, were not quite so far behindhand in their conclusions respecting it. That actually their "enthusiasms," if well seen into, were not foolish but wise. That Machiavelism, Cant, Official Jargon, whereby a man speaks openly what he does *not* mean, were, surprising as it may seem, much rarer then than they have ever since been. Really and truly it may in a manner be said, Cant, Parliamentary and other Jargon, were still to invent in this world. O Heavens, one could weep at the contrast! Cant was not fashionable at all; that stupendous invention of "Speech for the purpose of concealing Thought" was not yet made. A man wagging the tongue of him, as if it were the clapper of a bell to be rung for economic purposes, and not so much as attempting to convey any inner thought, if thought he have, of the matter talked of—would at that date have awakened all the horror in men's minds, which at all dates, and at this date too, is due to him. The accursed thing! No man as yet dared to do it; all men believing that God would judge them. In the History of the Civil War far and wide, I have not fallen in with one such phenomenon. . . .

The use of the human tongue was then other than it now is. I counsel the reader to leave all that of Cant, Dupery, Machiavelism, and so forth, decisively lying at the threshold. He will be wise to believe that these Puritans do mean what they say, and to try unimpeded if he can discover what that is. Gradually a very stupendous phenomenon may rise on his astonished eye. A practical world based on Belief in God;— such as many centuries had seen before, but as never any century since has been privileged to see. It was the last glimpse of it in our world, this of English Puri-

tanism: very great, very glorious; tragical enough to all thinking hearts that look on it from these days of ours.

My second advice is, Not to imagine that it was Constitution, "Liberty of the people to tax themselves," Privilege of Parliament, Triennial or annual Parliaments, or any modification of these sublime Privileges now waxing somewhat faint in our admirations, that mainly animated our Cromwells, Pyms, and Hampdens to the heroic efforts we still admire in retrospect. Not these very measurable "Privileges," but a far other and deeper, which could not be measured; of which these, and all grand social improvements whatsoever, are the corollary. Our ancient Puritan Reformers were, as all Reformers that will ever much benefit this Earth are always, inspired by a Heavenly Purpose. To see God's own Law, then universally acknowledged for complete as it stood in the holy Written Book, made good in this world; to see this, or the true unwearied aim and struggle towards this: it was a thing worth living for and dying for! Eternal Justice; that God's Will *be* done on Earth as it is in Heaven: corollaries enough will flow from that, if that be there; if that be not there, no corollary good for much will flow. It was the general spirit of England in the Seventeenth century. In other somewhat sadly disfigured form, we have seen the same immortal hope take practical shape in the French Revolution, and once more astonish the world. That England should all become a Church, if you like to name it so: a Church, presided over not by sham-priests in "Four surplices at Allhallowtide," but by true god-consecrated ones, whose hearts the Most High had touched and hallowed with his fire:— this was the prayer of many, it was the godlike hope and effort of some.

Our modern methods of Reform differ somewhat,—as indeed the issue testifies. I will advise my reader to forget the modern methods of Reform; not to remember that he has ever heard of a modern individual called by the name of Reformer, if he would understand what the old meaning of the word was. The Cromwells, Pyms, Hampdens, who were understood on the Royalist side to be firebrands of the Devil, have had still worse measure from the Dryasdust Philosophies, and sceptical Histories, of later times. They really did resemble firebrands of the Devil, if you looked at them through spectacles of a certain colour. For fire is always fire. But by no spectacles, only by mere blinders and *wooden-eyed* spectacles, can the flame-girt Heaven's-messenger pass for a poor mouldy Pedant and Constitution-monger, such as this would make him out to be!

On the whole, say not, good reader, as is often done, "It was then all one as now." Good reader, it was considerably different then from now. Men indolently say, "The Ages are all alike; ever the same sorry elements over again, in new vesture; the issue of it always a melancholy farce-tragedy, in one Age as in another!" Wherein lies very obviously a truth; but also in secret a very sad error withal. Sure enough, the highest Life touches always, by large sections of it, on the vulgar and universal: he that expects to see a Hero, or a Heroic Age, step forth into practice in yellow Drury-lane stage-boots, and speak in blank verse for itself, will look long in vain. Sure enough, in the Heroic Century as in the Unheroic, knaves and cowards, and cunning greedy persons were not wanting—were, if you will, extremely abundant. But the question always remains, Did they lie chained, subordinate in this world's business; coerced by steel-whips, or in whatever other effectual way, and sent whimpering into their due subterranean abodes, to beat hemp and repent; a true never-ending attempt going on to handcuff, to silence and suppress them? Or did they walk openly abroad, the envy of a general valet-population, and bear sway; professing, without universal anathema, almost with general assent, that they were the Or-thodox Party, that they, even they, were such men as you had right to look for?

Reader, the Ages differ greatly, even infinitely, from one another. Consider-able tracts of Ages there have been, by far the majority indeed, wherein the men, unfortunate mortals, were a set of mimetic creatures rather than men; without heart-insight as to this Universe, and its Heights and its Abysses; without conviction or belief of their own re-garding it, at all;—who walked merely by hearsays, traditionary cants, black and white surplices, and inane confu-sions;—whose whole Existence accord-ingly was a grimace; nothing *original* in it, nothing genuine or sincere but this only, Their greediness of appetite and their faculty of digestion. Such unhappy Ages, too numerous here below, the Genius of Mankind indig-nantly seizes, as disgraceful to the Fam-ily, and with Rhadamanthine ruthlessness —annihilates; tumbles large masses of them swiftly into eternal Night. These are the Unheroic Ages; which cannot serve, on the general field of Existence, except as *dust,* as inorganic manure. The memory of such Ages fades away for ever out of the minds of all men. Why should any memory of *them* continue? The fashion of them has passed away; and as for genuine substance, they never had any. To no heart of a man any more can these Ages become lovely. What melodious loving heart will search into *their* records, will sing of them, or celebrate them? Even torpid Dryasdust is forced to give over at last, all creatures declining to hear him on that subject; whereupon ensues composure and silence, and Oblivion has her own.

Good reader, if you be wise, search not for the secret of Heroic Ages, which have done great things in this Earth, among their falsities, their greedy quackeries and *un*heroisms! It never lies and never will lie there. Knaves and quacks —alas, we know they abounded: but the Age was Heroic even because it had declared war to the death with these, and would have neither truce nor treaty with these; and went forth, flame-crowned, as with bared sword, and called the Most High to witness that it would not endure these!

From of old, I will confess, this theory of Cromwell's falsity has been incredible to me. Nay I cannot believe the like, of any Great Man whatever. Multitudes of Great Men figure in History as false selfish men; but if we will consider it, they are but *figures* for us, unintelligible shadows; we do not see into them as men that could have existed at all. A superficial unbelieving generation only, with no eye but for the surfaces and semblances of things, could form such notions of Great Men. Can a great soul be possible without a *conscience* in it, the essence of all *real* souls, great or small?—No, we cannot figure Cromwell as a Falsity and Fatuity; the longer I study him and his career, I believe this the less. Why should we? There is no evidence of it. Is it not strange that, after all the mountains of calumny this man has been subject to, after being represented as the very prince of liars, who

never, or hardly ever, spoke truth, but always some cunning counterfeit of truth, there should not yet have been one falsehood brought clearly home to him? A prince of liars, and no lie spoken by him. Not one that I could yet get sight of. . . .

Looking at the man's life with our own eyes, it seems to me, a very different hypothesis suggests itself. What little we know of his earlier obscure years, distorted as it has come down to us, does it not all betoken an earnest, affectionate, sincere kind of man? His nervous melancholic temperament indicates rather a seriousness *too* deep for him. Of those stories of 'Spectres'; of the white Spectre in broad daylight, predicting that he should be King of England, we are not bound to believe much—probably no more than of the other black Spectre, or Devil in person, to whom the Officer *saw* him sell himself before Worcester Fight! But the mournful, over-sensitive, hypochondriac humour of Oliver, in his young years, is otherwise indisputably known. . . . These things are significant. Such an excitable deep-feeling nature, in that rugged stubborn strength of his, is not the symptom of falsehood; it is the symptom and promise of quite other than falsehood!

His successes in Parliament, his successes through the war, are honest successes of a brave man; who has more resolution in the heart of him, more light in the head of him than other men. His prayers to God; his spoken thanks to the God of Victory, who had preserved him safe, and carried him forward so far, through the furious clash of a world all set in conflict, through desperate-looking envelopments at Dunbar; through the death-hail of so many battles; mercy after mercy; to the 'crowning mercy' of Worcester Fight: all this is good and genuine for a deep-hearted

Calvinistic Cromwell. Only to vain unbelieving Cavaliers, worshipping not God but their own 'love-locks,' frivolities and formalities, living quite apart from contemplations of God, living *without* God in the world, need it seem hypocritical.

Nor will his participation in the King's death involve him in condemnation with us. It is a stern business killing of a King! But if you once go to war with him, it lies *there;* this and all else lies there. Once at war, you have made wager of battle with him: it is he to die, or else you. Reconciliation is problematic; may be possible, or, far more likely, is impossible. It is now pretty generally admitted that the Parliament, having vanquished Charles First, had no way of making any tenable arrangement with him. The large Presbyterian party, apprehensive now of the Independents, were most anxious to do so; anxious indeed as for their own existence; but it could not be. The unhappy Charles, in those final Hampton-Court negotiations, shows himself as a man fatally incapable of being dealt with. A man who, once for all, could not and would not *understand:*—whose thought did not in any measure represent to him the real fact of the matter; nay worse, whose *word* did not at all represent his thought. We may say this of him without cruelty, with deep pity rather: but it is true and undeniable. Forsaken there of all but the *name* of Kingship, he still, finding himself treated with outward respect as a King, fancied that he might play off party against party, and smuggle himself into his old power by deceiving both. Alas, they both *discovered* that he was deceiving them. A man whose *word* will not inform you at all what he means or will do, is not a man you can bargain with. You must get out of that man's way, or put him out of yours! The Presbyterians, in their despair, were still for believing Charles, though found false, unbelievable again and again. Not so Cromwell: "For all our fighting," says he, "we are to have a little bit of paper?" No!—

In fact, everywhere we have to note the decisive practical *eye* of this man; how he drives towards the practical and practicable; has a genuine insight into what *is* fact. Such an intellect. I maintain, does not belong to a false man: the false man sees false shows, plausibilities, expediences: the true man is needed to discern even practical truth. Cromwell's advice about the Parliament's Army, early in the contest, How they were to dismiss their city-tapsters, flimsy riotous persons, and choose substantial yeomen, whose heart was in the work, to be soldiers for them: this is advice by a man who *saw*. Fact answers, if you see into Fact! Cromwell's *Ironsides* were the embodiment of this insight of his; men fearing God; and without any other fear. No more conclusively genuine set of fighters ever trod the soil of England, or of any other land.

Neither will we blame greatly that word of Cromwell's to them; which was so blamed: "If the King should meet me in battle, I would kill the King." Why not? These words were spoken to men who stood as before a Higher than Kings. They had set more than their own lives on the cast. The Parliament may call it, in official language, a fighting *'for the King';* but we, for our share, cannot understand that. To us it is no dilettante work, no sleek officiality; it is sheer rough death and earnest. They have brought it to the calling-forth of *War;* horrid internecine fight, man grappling with man in fire-eyed rage,—the *infernal* element in man called forth, to try it by that! *Do* that therefore; since that is the thing to be done. — The successes of Cromwell seem to me a very natural thing! Since he was not shot in battle, they were an inevitable thing. That such a man, with the eye to see, with the heart to dare, should advance, from post to post, from victory to victory, till the Huntingdon Farmer became, by whatever name you might call him, the acknowledged Strongest Man in England, virtually the King of England, requires no magic to explain it! —

Truly it is a sad thing for a people, as for a man, to fall into Scepticism, into dilettantism, insincerity; not to know a Sincerity when they see it. For this world, and for all worlds, what curse is so fatal? The heart lying dead, the eye cannot see. What intellect remains is merely the *vulpine* intellect. That a true *King* be sent them is of small use; they do not know him when sent. They say scornfully, Is this your King? The Hero wastes his heroic faculty in bootless contradiction from the unworthy; and can accomplish little. For himself he does accomplish a heroic life, which is much, which is all; but for the world he accomplishes comparatively nothing. The wild rude Sincerity, direct from Nature, is not glib in answering from the witness-box: in your small-debt *piepowder* court, he is scouted as a counterfeit. The vulpine intellect 'detects' him. For being a man worth any thousand men, the response your Knox, your Cromwell gets, is an argument for two centuries whether he was a man at all. God's greatest gift to this Earth is sneeringly flung away. The miraculous talisman is a paltry plated coin, not fit to pass in the shops as a common guinea.

Lamentable this! I say, this must be remedied. Till this be remedied in some measure, there is nothing remedied. 'Detect quacks'? Yes do, for Heaven's sake; but know withal the men that are to be trusted! . . . The world does exist; the world has truth in it, or it would not exist! First recognise what is true, we we shall *then* discern what is false; and properly never till then.

'Know the men that are to be trusted': alas, this is yet, in these days, very far from us. The sincere alone can recognise sincerity. Not a Hero only is needed, but a world fit for him; a world not of *Valets;* —the Hero comes almost in vain to it otherwise! Yes, it is far from us: but it must come; thank God, it is visibly coming. Till it do come, what have we? Ballot-boxes, suffrages, French Revolutions:—if we are as Valets, and do not know the Hero when we see him, what good are all these? A heroic Cromwell comes; and for a hundred and fifty years he cannot have a vote from us. Why, the insincere, unbelieving world is the *natural property* of the Quack, and of the Father of quacks and quackeries! Misery, confusion, unveracity are alone possible there. By ballot-boxes we alter the *figure* of our Quack; but the substance of him continues. The Valet-World *has* to be governed by the Sham-Hero, by the King merely *dressed* in King-gear. It is his; he is its! In brief, one of two things: We shall either learn to know a Hero, a true Governor and Captain, somewhat better, when we see him; or else go on to be forever governed by the Unheroic;—had we ballot-boxes clattering at every street-corner, there were no remedy in these.

Poor Cromwell, — great Cromwell! The inarticulate Prophet; Prophet who could not *speak.* Rude, confused, struggling to utter himself, with his savage depth, with his wild sincerity; and he looked so strange, among the elegant Euphemisms, dainty little Falklands, didactic Chillingworths, diplomatic

Clarendons! Consider him. An outer hull of chaotic confusion, visions of the Devil, nervous dreams, almost semi-madness; and yet such a clear determinate man's energy working in the heart of that. A kind of chaotic man. The ray as of pure starlight and fire, working in such an element of boundless hypochondria, *un*formed black of darkenss! And yet withal this hypochondria, what was it but the very greatness of the man? The depth and tenderness of his wild affections: the quantity of *sympathy* he had with things—the quantity of insight he would yet get into the heart of things, the mastery he would yet get over things: this was his hypochondria. The man's misery, as man's misery always does, came of his greatness. . . . Sorrow-stricken, half-distracted; the wide element of mournful *black* enveloping him,—wide as the world. It is the character of a prophetic man; a man with his whole soul *seeing,* and struggling to see.

On this ground, too, I explain to myself Cromwell's reputed confusion of speech. To himself the internal meaning was sun-clear; but the material with which he was to clothe it in utterance was not there. He had *lived* silent; a great unnamed sea of Thought round him all his days; and in his way of life little call to attempt *naming* or uttering that. With his sharp power of vision, resolute power of action, I doubt not he could have learned to write Books withal, and speak fluently enough;—he did harder things than writing of Books. This kind of man is precisely he who is fit for doing manfully all things you will set him on doing. Intellect is not speaking and logicising; it is seeing and ascertaining. Virtue, *Vir-tus,* manhood, *hero*-hood, is not fair-spoken immaculate regularity; it is first of all, what the Germans well name it, *Tugend* (*Taugend, dow*-ing or *Dough*-tiness), Courage and the Faculty to *do.* This basis of the matter Cromwell had in him. . . .

But indeed his actual Speeches, I apprehend, were not nearly so ineloquent, incondite, as they look. We find he was, what all speakers aim to be, an impressive speaker, even in Parliament; one who, from the first, had weight. With that rude passionate voice of his, he was always understood to *mean* something, and men wished to know what. He disregarded eloquence, nay despised and disliked it; spoke always without premeditation of the words he was to use. The Reporters, too, in those days seem to have been singularly candid; and to have given the Printer precisely what they found on their own notepaper. And withal, what a strange proof is it of Cromwell's being the premeditative ever-calculating hypocrite, acting a play before the world, That to the last he took no more charge of his Speeches! How came he not to study his words a little, before flinging them out to the public? If the words were true words, they could be left to shift for themselves. . . .

Cromwell, no doubt of it, spoke often in the dialect of small subaltern parties; uttered to them a *part* of his mind. Each little party thought him all its own. Hence their rage, one and all, to find him not of their party, but of his own party! Was it his blame? At all seasons of his history he must have felt, among such people, how, if he explained to them the deeper insight he had, they must either have shuddered aghast at it, or believing it, their own little compact hypothesis must have gone wholly to wreck. They could not have worked in his province any more; nay perhaps they could not now have worked in their own province.

It is the inevitable position of a great man among small men.

Oliver is gone; and with him England's Puritanism, laboriously built together by this man, and made a thing far-shining miraculous to its own Century, and memorable to all the Centuries, soon goes. Puritanism, without its King, is *kingless,* anarchic; falls into dislocation, self-collision; staggers, plunges into ever deep anarchy; King, Defender of the Puritan Faith there can now none be found; and nothing is left but to recall the old disowned Defender, with the remnants of his Four Surplices, and two Centuries of *Hypocrisia,* and put up with all that, the best we may. The Genius of England no longer soars Sunward, world-defiant, like an eagle through the storms, "mewing her mighty youth," as John Milton saw her do: the Genius of England, much liker a greedy Ostrich intent on provender and a whole skin mainly, stands with its *other* extremity Sunward; with its Ostrich-head stuck into the readiest bush, of old Church-tippets, King-cloaks, or what other "sheltering Fallacy" there may be, and *so* awaits the issue. The issue has been slow; but it is now seen to have been inevitable. No ostrich, intent on gross terrene provender, and sticking its head into Fallacies, but will be awakened one day,—in a terrible *a*-*posteriori* manner, if not otherwise!—Awake before it come to that: gods and men bid us awake! The Voices of our Fathers, with thousandfold stern monition to one and all, bid us awake.

Better known for his gripping adventure stories than for his masterly historical biographies, JOHN BUCHAN, First Baron Tweedsmuir (1875–1940), was a member of Parliament, then in 1935 a peer and Governor-General of Canada. As the son of a Scottish minister, educated at Glasgow and Oxford, he was always a devout Christian, an ardent imperialist, and admirer of the relatively closed upper circle in Britain. His faith, ardor, and admiration for British vigor informed his novels and history alike. His rich experience, when brought to bear on Cromwell, resulted in a stylish and persuasive biography.*

John Buchan

The Ordinary Englishman

The basic stuff of Oliver's character was the same as that of the ordinary English countryman, of more delicate texture than most, and interwoven with finer strands, but essentially the same tough workaday fabric. He had none of the leaden arrogance of the superman who seeks a pedestal apart from humanity. Though pinnacled high enough by fate, he was never out of hearing of the common voices of life. Nature had made him all for peace, Marvell said, anticipating Wordsworth's picture of the happy warrior. The leaning of his master-bias was always "to homefelt pleasures and to gentle scenes."

He was greatly dependent upon family affection, giving much and receiving much. He could not bear to be long out of the household circle, and dined and supped with it even in the thick of his heaviest cares. Only one member can be said to have really influenced him, his mother, whom, till she died at a great age, he visited every night before he went to bed. She had done much to form him, but she was a little awed at her handiwork, and her pride in him was tempered by a constant anxiety about his safety. His wife Elizabeth was also a careful mortal, who struggled hard with honours to which she had not been born, and tried to forget the great lady in the prudent housewife. She did her best to live up to his state, but as a ceremonial figure she may have lacked something, for Lucy Hutchinson says that grandeur sat as ill on her as

---

* From John Buchan, *Oliver Cromwell* (London, 1934) pp. 510–525. Used by permission of the Trustees of the Tweedsmuir estate, *per* A. P. Watt and Son, London, W.C. 2, literary agents, and the publishers, Hodder and Stoughton Ltd., London, E.C. 4.

scarlet on an ape. But she acquired unexpected tastes, one of which was a little picture gallery of her own, for we find her asking foreign ambassadors for portraits of their countries' notables.

Six grown-up children made up the Protector's household; two boys had died long ago, and he never forgot them. Richard, the eldest surviving son, had thrown back to the Huntingdon squires— Lucy Hutchinson will have it to the Huntingdon peasants. He was a plain country gentleman, not without brains and breeding, but sluggish except in sport, careless about his affairs, and wholly wanting in ambition. Henry was of another stamp, for his work in Ireland showed that he could handle men, and his letters to Thurloe prove that he had no small share of political wisdom. Oliver's attitude towards his sons was characteristic. He was deeply concerned about their spiritual state, and was always in fear lest indulgence on his part should mar their characters. His letters to them, for all their tenderness, are a little school-masterish in tone. He did not quite realize that they had grown up, even when Henry had given proof of his competence.

A masterful father is often happiest with his daughters, and certainly the Cromwell girls were not unworthy of him. Their portraits show them as comely young women, their faces a little heavy in the lower part, but redeemed by fine brows and compelling eyes. The carriage of their heads has a notable dignity. All talked and wrote the language of Zion, like dutiful children, but cheerfulness often broke into their piety, not wholly to their father's displeasure. . . .

Having become ruler of England and prince in all but name, Oliver's sturdy good sense made him resolved to keep up a state worthy of his dignity. He succeded in combining the intimacies of family life with the splendour of a court—"a court of sin and vanity," its critic croaks, "and the more abominable because they had not yet quite cast away the name of God, but profaned it by taking it in vain among them." It was indeed a curious mixture of pageantry and piety, but the blend was impressive, the velvet glove with the hardness of steel behind it, the silken mantle over armour. There were interminable sermons—three hours when John Howe preached—and multitudinous lengthy prayers, and there was always a psalm at the supper parties. There were fast days when a sabbath calm filled the palace. But the ceremonial occasions were managed high and disposedly, for, as his bitterest critics confessed, Oliver "had much natural greatness and well became the place he had usurped." He had one hundred thousand pounds to spend annually on his household, and, though he gave away at least a third of this in charity, he used the remainder well. He had his scarlet-coated lifeguards, and, apart from lackeys, some fifty gentlemen about his person clad in uniforms of black and grey with silver trimmings. He kept a good table, and his guests could taste the first pineapples ever brought to England. His own diet was plain English fare with no foreign kickshaws, and his drink was a light wine or a very small ale.

His one indoor hobby was music. At Hampton Court he had two organs, and at Whitehall a variety of instruments. Whenever he gave a dinner, whether to foreign ambassadors or parliament men or members of Council, he had music played throughout the evening. He loved the human voice and had a taste for glees and part-songs, in which he took a share. For art he had respect, and he saved the Raphael cartoons for England, but he had little knowledge of it; his inclination seems to have been towards realism, for he bade Lely in painting his portrait re-produce all the roughnesses of his face. There is no evidence that he read much, or indeed anything, beyond the Bible, but he had a kindness for men of letters and protected even those who opposed him, and he was a painstaking chancellor of Oxford.

To the end of his life he remained the countryman, and his happiest hours were spent in the long weekends at Hampton Court, where he had constructed fish-ponds and inclosed a warren. That was the sole relaxation permitted him, for the times were too critical to go far from London. The only game he played was bowls, but in field sports he had a most catholic taste. Hawking had been the amusement of his earlier days and he never lost his zest for it. Old, out-at-elbows, cavalier falconers won his favour, and he did his best to entice away Whitelocke's servant who had good skill in hawks. But hawking demanded a freedom of movement and a leisure which he did not possess, and as Protector he had few opportunities for it beyond an occasional day on Hounslow Heath. So also with hunting, another pastime of his youth. Marvell speaks of

> his delight
> In horses fierce, wild deer, or armour bright.

His love of the dun deer was famous, and Queen Christina of Sweden collected as a present for him a small herd of reindeer, which was unfortunately destroyed by wolves before it could be despatched to England. As Protector he had to confine his indulgence in the chase to the park at Hampton Court, where after dinner he would sometimes course a buck, and amaze the foreign ambassadors by his bold jumping.

Horses were his abiding passion. He suppressed bear-baiting and cock-fighting because of their cruelty, but his prohibi-tion of horse-racing was only local and temporary, and due solely to its political danger as an excuse for royalist meetings. The old cavalry leader was the best judge of a horse in England. There is no evidence that he raced himself, but his stud was his delight, and he laboured to improve the breed. We hear of his well-matched coach-teams—reddish-grey and snow-white—better, said rumour, than any king of England had ever possessed. The Godolphin Barb and the Darley Arabian had their predecessors in his stables, and every English agent on the Mediterranean shores held a roving commission from the Protector. He bought barbs in Tripoli and arabs in Aleppo, for he had had enough of the heavy Flanders brand and knew that what the English stock wanted was the fineness of the East. At one crisis of his life, when a deputation from parliament visited him on the matter of the crown, he kept it waiting for two hours while he inspected a barb in the garden. This constant touch with the natural world was one of his rare founts of refreshment. It was a link with the old simple country life for which he always hankered, and it kept him in tune with his fellow-men. A spirit, which otherwise might have lost itself in aerial flights, had this wholesome tether to English soil.

Of his manner and bearing we have many accounts, which in substance agree. He had a quick temper and from his boy-hood had been liable to bursts of wrath. He was a hero to his steward John Maid-ston, who wrote candidly of him that his "temper was exceeding fiery, as I have known, but the flame of it kept down for the most part, or soon allayed, with those moral endowments he had." Now and then, as we have seen, passion got the upper hand to his own undoing, but of such bouts he always repented. A temper held in curb is a useful possession for a ruler, for it is no bad thing for the world to realize that somewhere there are banked fires. This high spirit well bitted gave him a fine stateliness on the proper occasions, for all observers are agreed on what Sir Philip Warwick called his "great and majestic deportment." But this majesty was not habitual, for pride was no part of his philosophy; rather he held it a sin. He was the most accessible of men, labouring to be conciliatory and to understand another's point of view.

For he no duty by his height excused,
Nor, though a prince, to be a man refused.

He had no egotism, and would readily take advice and allow himself to be persuaded. He would even permit opponents to enlarge on his faults and point out his spiritual defects, than which there can be no greater proof of humility.

Yet his brooding power and the sense of slumbering flames would, in spite of his patient courtesy, have repelled most men but for another endowment which impressed all who came into his company. He radiated an infinite kindliness. Here was one who hated harshness and cruelty, and who loved, and would fain be loved by, his fellows. "He was naturally compassionate towards objects in distress," says Maidston, "even to an effeminate measure." In war he had been notably merciful; in peace he had a heart that felt for all suffering and squandered almost too readily its affection. Marvell is the best witness, Marvell who had a poet's insight, and who had watched him often in the Council chamber and in the privacy of his family. The key-note of Marvell's memorial verses is the "wondrous softness of his heart."

His tenderness extended unto all.
And that deep soul through every channel flows
Where kindly Nature loves itself to lose.
More strong affections never reason served.

They did not always serve reason; that was their peculiar charm; they often defied logic and good sense and prudence, being no bridled and calculated things but the overflow of a deep loving-kindness. There is one illuminating phrase of the poet's, when he looks at the dead Protector and laments that those eyes are closed which once shed "a piercing sweetness." Here, more than in his moments of Sinaitic awe, lay the secret of Oliver's power over men. The doubter, who had not been persuaded by his wordy and halting arguments, saw suddenly the stern face, roughened by weather and lined by care, transformed into a strange beauty. A great mercy, a wistful tenderness looked out of the eyes. The critic went away a disciple, for he had had a glimpse of something divine.

Oliver's mind was like a powerful mill which avidly took in grist but which ground slowly and fitfully. He had no deft logical mechanism always at his command. One talent he possessed in the highest degree, the perceptive, the power of recognizing and appreciating facts. Unlike many religious men of his day he did not rely upon divine admonitions, having a wholesome contempt for those who construed their own private whims as the voice of God. God worked through events, providences, facts, and it was in them that men should read His will. But the puzzle lay in interpreting these concrete celestial messages, for it was not enough to recognize their urgency, since from them a rule of action must be drawn and a philosophy of conduct. He generalized, as we have seen, with extreme difficulty. Texts of Scripture assisted him. Ireton had been a wonderful clarifier of his mind, and now and then he got help from divines like Howe and Sterry and from wise laymen like Whitelocke and Thurloe. But for the most part he did his own theorizing, and his cloudy trophies were hardly won. There was nothing in him of the doctrinaire, for his experience and reflection did not easily shape themselves into dogmas, and never into formulas. But painfully over long tracts of time a policy would distil itself, which was no more than a working rule, for a change of circumstances might compel him to revise it. In these processes there was little formal reasoning, though when it was necessary he could argue acutely. Unconscious instinct played a larger part than ratiocination. He was made in the traditional mould of Englishmen, and had behind him all the centuries of England—the dreams of Langland, the ripe wisdom of Chaucer, the radicalism of Wycliffe, the conservatism of the lawyers, the peasant's kinship with the earth, the Elizabethan adventurers' open eyes and insurgent hearts. Much that was hoar-ancient crept into the substance of his thought.

Few minds have had a more invincible candour. "A soldier disciplined to perfection in the knowledge of himself," Milton called him, and he was altogether free from the lie in the soul. Such candour involves inconsistency, for consistency is usually the product of either obtuseness or vanity. No man was ever more extravagantly inconsistent. Between 1653 and 1658 he tried five systems of government —a military dictatorship; a dictatorship with a picked parliament; a dictatorship with a written instrument; a military dictatorship again; a quasi-constitutional monarchy. His inconsistency extended into those matters where politics and morals meet. He did everything—and more—that the men he had broken had done, and repeated the very offences for which he had opposed them. He taxed

the people more highly and disregarded parliament more brazenly than Charles; he treated Ireland more cavalierly than Strafford; he interfered with personal liberty more tyrannously than Laud. It was easy for his enemies, both of his own and later ages, to present him as a man of a cool and insatiable ambition, who had calculated every step and allowed no moralities to stand in his way. Such an explanation is too simple, and it is incompatible both with a great body of evidence, and with the structure of human nature; but superficially it was not without its warrant. As we have seen, he always desired to persuade rather than to compel, and his persuasion was often not far from cajolery, for to different people he would use different and contradictory pleas. If he did not lie, he sometimes acted a lie, and the charge of duplicity was not always unfounded. "If a man is not a good, sound, honest, capable liar," Samuel Butler has written, "there is no truth in him," and assuredly the truth that was in Oliver was not a pedantic fidelity to the letter.

To understand him we must remember that he was first and foremost a man of a crisis, struggling to put together again that which fate had broken. For such a task opportunism is the most necessary virtue, an eye for changing facts and a readiness to change with them. The oddest charge ever levelled against him is that of fanaticism; on the contrary he was the hammer of fanatics, one who turned unhesitatingly to the instant need of things. If the poet is right and

> to know all naked truths,
> And to envisage circumstances, all calm,
> That is the top of sovereignty—

then he was born to rule. His success in war had been largely due to the fact that he never worked by a preconceived plan, but let events shape his course for him, and he carried the same principle into statecraft. "He could vary the methods with which he combated each evil of the day as it arose. Those who attached themselves to him in his struggle against the King, or against the different Parliaments of his time, or against the military power, were as incapable as he was capable of facing round to confront each danger as it arose. From the moment that each partial victory was won, the old friends had to be reasoned with, then discarded, and at last restrained from doing mischief." His working rule was that of Marchamont Needham; government was "an art or artifice found out by man's wisdom and occasioned by necessity," and not a deduction from "principles of natural right and freedom." He had as deep a contempt for the compact and riveted logic of the republican and the leveller as for the fantasies of the Fifth Monarchy men. His mind was wholly unspeculative, and he never felt the compulsion which others have felt to weave his views into an harmonious system of thought.

It was impossible for him, being the man he was, to leave any permanent construction behind him, any more than he could leave a code of principles. He was the creature of emergencies, and he died while he was still feeling his way. England, let it be remembered, blundered and sidled into modern parliamentarism. Oliver more than any other of her historic rulers had the hard bourgeois sense of reality, and he decided that Pym's notions simply would not work. In that he was right. The spirit of the Restoration was largely negative; certain old things disappeared for ever, but it took several generations, and many false starts, to frame a system which combined expert administration with a measure of popular control. Something in the nature of a permanent civil service had first to be created.

But if Oliver left nothing that endured, no more did the Vanes and Ludlows who opposed him. . . .

Oliver stands out in history as the great improviser, desperately trying expedient after expedient, and finding every tool cracking in his hand. He dies, the experiments cease, and there is a fatigued return to the old ways. But it is possible to discover in that cloudy mind an ideal of the State which he was not fated to realize, but which he did not cease to cherish. Dryden had a glimmering of this when he wrote in his memorial verses,

Poor mechanic arts in public move,
Whilst the deep secrets beyond practice go.

Like Caesar, another man of a crisis, we must judge him not only by his actual work but by his ultimate purpose, the substance of things hoped for.

His profoundest conviction, which on occasion could make him tender even towards the zealots of the Fifth Monarchy, was that government should be in the hands of the good and wise, of those whom he thought of as the people of God. For the fundamental tenet of plebiscitary democracy, the virtue of a majority of counted heads, he had only contempt. The justification of such a method on the ground of practical convenience—its only serious justification—would have seemed to him a sin against the divine purpose. The mechanism of the ballot-box was no more to him than a child's toy. He believed in government by the general will, but he did not define that as the will of all. The essence of common democracy is quantity, and he desired quality. The mind was the man, he told parliament; with an impure mind man was no better than a beast, and a beast could not rule:

the State must be controlled by the seeing eyes and the single hearts.

But to this conviction he added another, which made him a democrat of an extreme type in his ultimate ideals. His religion taught him the transcendent value of every immortal soul, even though dwelling in the humblest body. He dreamed of an aristocracy of quality where the best would govern, but all would be the best. The State he thought of as, in Kant's words, "a kingdom of ends, where all are sovereign because all are subjects." His zeal for education and for the faithful preaching of the Word is the practical proof of a belief which appears in broken gleams everywhere in his speeches and letters. He was no leveller to seek a monotonous, unfeatured community. He believed in diversity of station—noble, squire, yeoman, merchant and peasant—as congenial to human nature and as giving stability to society, but he would have made each class a partner in the duties and a sharer in the rights of the English polity. His toleration was based on the same principle, that variety of emphasis in faith tended to strengthen the spiritual life of a nation. Tolerance ultimately triumphed through the cynics and sceptics who taught that such differences were trivial, and therefore negligible; Oliver with a brave optimism stood for them because of their value. His one exception proved his rule, for he was chary about popery because it was of its nature to press "from an equality to a superiority." Liberty was his ultimate goal, the liberty of God's people, where all were free because all were servants of the same high purpose, and Milton was not wrongly inspired when he hailed him as *patriae liberator, libertatis creator, custoque idem et conservator.*†

—————
†Liberator of the country, founder of freedom, keeper & conservator of the same—Ed.

But liberty to him meant not a mechanic thing measured out in statutory doses, still less a disordered license, but the joyous collaboration of those whom the truth had made free, "a partnership," in Burke's great words, "in every virtue and in all perfection."

He summoned his country to an *ascesis* which was beyond its power, and certainly beyond its desires. England turned to another creed—a minimum of government and that government a thing of judicious checks and balances. It was the doctrine of Montrose, the other great idealist of the age, that won the day. The satiety with high communal, as with high spiritual, dreams permitted men to devote themselves to their own concerns, and in the next two hundred years to build up a national life founded upon a rich and strenuous individualism, with the State guarding the ring and charging a modest entrance fee. In the quasi-democratic creed of these centuries Oliver had no part, for it was based upon quantity not quality, enumeration not evaluation, arithmetic not philosophy. He did not fail to establish democracy, as some have said. He failed in a far greater task, to create a spiritualized and dedicated nation. . . .

But his bequest to the world was not institutions, for his could not last, or a political faith, for his was more instinct and divination than coherent thought. It was the man himself, in his good and ill, his frailty and his strength, typical in almost every quality of his own English people, but with these qualities so magnified as to become epic and universal. He belongs to the small circle of great kings, though he never sat on a throne; like Milton's Adam,

in himself was all his state
More solemn than the tedious pomp that waits
On princes.

His figure still radiates an immortal energy. "Their distinction," Burke has written of him and his kind, "was not so much like men usurping power as asserting their natural place in society. Their rising was to illuminate and beautify the world. Their conquest over their competitors was by outshining them. The hand that like a destroying angel smote the country communicated to it the force and energy under which it suffered." Though he wrought in a narrower field and influenced far less profoundly the destinies of mankind, and though in sheer intellect he was manifestly their inferior, he had the same power as Caesar and Napoleon, the gift of forcing facts to serve him, of compelling multitudes of men into devotion or acquiescence.

But it is on that point alone that he is kin to those cyclopean architects and roadmakers, the world's conquerors. Almost without exception they were spirits of an extreme ambition, egotism and pride, holding aloof from the kindly race of men. Oliver remained humble, homely, with a ready sympathy and goodwill. For, while he was winning battles and dissolving parliaments and carrying the burdens of a people, he was living an inner life so intense that, compared with it, the outer world was the phantasmagoria of a dream. There is no parallel in history to this iron man of action whose consuming purpose was at all times the making of his soul.

WILBUR CORTEZ ABBOTT (1869–1947) did graduate work at Cornell and completed his education at Oxford and on the continent. A trail of university posts led him finally to Harvard. He was an accomplished essayist with wide-ranging interests, but his greatest labors were lavished on Cromwell. Like Carlyle, he set himself to edit all Cromwell's extant writings and speeches. Very little escaped his eye and his edition is regarded as definitive because it was fuller, more accurate, and up-to-date than Carlyle's. Abbott surrounded his primary evidence with a comprehensive narrative which was colored by his relativism and acute distaste for the emergence of dictatorships in his time. So Cromwell's infamy, for Abbott, was part and parcel of his fame.*

Wilbur Cortez Abbott

Hitler Illuminates Cromwell

One question remains concerning Oliver Cromwell, and that the most frequently asked and perhaps the most important of all questions about him. What kind of a man was he? . . . "What can be more extraordinary," said his contemporary, Cowley, "than that a person of private birth and education, no fortune, no eminent qualities of body, which have sometimes, nor shining qualities of mind, which have often, raised men to the highest dignities, should have the courage to attempt and the ability to execute so great a design as the subverting one of the most ancient and best established monarchies in the world?" He had accomplished the impossible. He had been granted that "marvellous distinction of breaking through the charmed circle which among European nations hems in the private man." In an age of divine right, this English squire became the ruler of three kingdoms, wielding an authority which had no precedent and no appropriate name. . . .

Grown to such greatness, he was admired rather than loved by his immediate followers; hated and feared, even when most respected, by his enemies. What his soldiers thought of him; what those voiceless thousands whose banner he bore believed, we can only surmise from their actions. His cofferer, Maidstone, declared that to him the Protector's head "seemed a storehouse and a shop of vast treasury of natural parts, his temper fiery but

*From W. C. Abbott, *The Writings and Speeches of Oliver Cromwell*, 4 vols. (Cambridge, Mass., 1937–47), IV, 877–899. Used by permission of the President and Fellows of Harvard College and Harvard University Press, Cambridge, Mass.

kept down . . . compassionate, fearless, a larger soule hath seldom dwelt in a house of clay; religious, yet his temptations were such as it appeared frequently that he who had grace enough for many men might have too little for himself, the treasure that he had being but an earthen vessel and that equally defiled with original sin as any other man's is"—an appreciation which the Protector might well have read with mingled amusement and humility.

Of whole-hearted literary defense by writers of first rank he had little enough in his own time, save that the greatest pen of Christendom was on his side. That counted for much, indeed—more in our day, perhaps, than in his own. To Milton at the outset of the great experiment of the Commonwealth he was

Cromwell our chief of men, who through a cloud
Not of war only, but detractions rude,
Guided by faith and matchless fortitude,
To peace and truth thy glorious way hath ploughed.

Yet even here the warning does not fail; already fear—or is it doubt?—intrudes.

　　. . . much remains
To conquer still: Peace hath her victories
No less renowned than war; new foes arise—

Two years later, when that experiment had failed, Milton's prose appeal to Cromwell to take the supreme power touched the high level of English eloquence. Yet when Commonwealth and Protectorate alike were over and the Protector dead, the great Puritan's pen was still. Not so that of the splendid sycophant, Dryden, who sang at the Protector's funeral—

His grandeur he derived from Heaven alone,
For he was great ere fortune made him so;
And wars, like mists that rise against the sun,
Made him but greater seem, not greater grow—

Even when royalty was restored Dryden spoke of him as that

. . . bold Typhoeus . . . who had scaled the sky,
And forced great Jove from his own Heaven to fly.

Yet, on the whole, that candid friend, Andrew Marvell, perhaps best expressed the more moderate view of his own party.

And well he therefore does, and well has guessed,
Who in his age has always forward pressed;
And knowing not where Heaven's choice may light,
Girds yet his sword, and ready stands to fight.
. . . .
He seems a king by long succession born,
And yet the same to be a king doth scorn;
Abroad a king he seems and something more,
At home a subject on the equal floor.

In the main, however, the record judgments of his contemporaries, when not mere libels or panegyrics or, as in Milton's case, identification of the Protector with a cause, were hostile or extremely critical. Nor is this surprising. His enemies were numerous, able and gifted in tongues; and, occupying as he did in later years, a middle ground, he was assailed on every side. First came the Presbyterians, who damned him with faint praise. . . . Fiercest of all were the Republicans, who felt themselves betrayed by this apostate to the Commonwealth, who had led them to the borders of the Promised Land only to seize it for himself. . . . The Royalists, however bitter, entertained no such fond imaginings of the perfectibility of human nature. "Had his cause been good," said Reresby, Cromwell would have ranked as "one of the greatest and bravest men the world ever produced." To Clarendon he had, it is true, "all the wickedness against which damnation is pronounced and for which hell-fire is prepared." Yet he had, too, "some virtues which have caused the memory of some men in all ages to be celebrated"; he was a tyrant, but not "a man of blood"; he had a "wonderful understanding in the natures and humours of men . . . a great spirit, an admirable circumspection and sagacity, and a most magnanimous resolution"; he was, in short, "a brave, bad man." . . .

Thus, under such widely varying auspices, the first stage of Cromwell's reputation came to an end with his death; and his fame, under such different aspects, set forth upon its long and chequered career.

Its first adventure was with the returned Royalism of the Restoration period; and scarcely had Church and Crown come to their own again when the long-pent flood of execration burst upon the tyrant's memory. . . . Heath's *Flagellum* . . . , long the most widely read of his biographies, allowed its subject no qualities save those of evil; vilified his family; accused him and them of all the basest vice and crime; pictured him as a monster no less despicable in private life than damnable in public action; and stripped him of every shred not merely of virtue and ability but of even common decency.

Now that reviling had become not only safe but profitable, it was small wonder that many lesser spirits were inspired. While the lighter-minded of the Royalists vented their feelings in a famous tavern-song which commemorated his fabled origin as a brewer and the splendid copper color of his nose, we may judge the hatred he inspired when even sober gentlemen like John Evelyn could record: "Died that arch-rebel called Protector . . . the joyfullest funeral I ever saw, for there were none that cried but dogs. . . .

This period of unchallenged invective was to last but six years. Then the Dutch fought the English on nearly equal terms; the English government by maladministration, extravagance, war, plague, and fire, was brought close to bankruptcy and put up its fleet; the Dutch sailed up the Thames; the unprotected English men-of-war were sunk or burned; London heard the thunder of Dutch guns, and every English port felt their insulting presence. And "It is strange," wrote Pepys, "how everybody do nowadays reflect upon Oliver and commend him, what brave things he did, and made all the neighbors fear him, while here a prince, come in with all the love and prayers and good liking of his people . . . hath lost all so soon." Thus his courage and ability which had made him what he was while he was alive, had begun to protect his memory once he was gone; for within a year the first defense of his rule appeared in print.

That reaction found no echo on the Continent. There, meanwhile, a Cromwell legend had arisen. It is significant that the most considerable writers who essayed his life were all Italians. The spirit in which they wrote is best expressed in the title of a later German work *Arcana Dominationis*—the secrets of governing. To Machiavelli's countrymen this was the chief appeal of the English Puritan, his mastery of men and of the "mysteries of state." Dear to the heart of earlier, empiric statesmanship, versed in the arts of management, and the means by which individual fortunes were advanced and subjects kept submissive, these were the lessons to be learned from this master of statecraft. . . . [Such spirit] was summed up in the most famous of this group, Gregorio Leti's *Life,* the longest account of the Protector which had yet appeared, and the one which largely determined the Continental conception of him for a century. . . .

In Leti's view Cromwell was a prodigy,

conceiving and executing the subversion of royalty with courage, ambition, and prudence; and compelling fortune by his marvelous ability. He dominated the most fiery, subdued the most obstinate. None knew better how to assume a mask of hypocrisy to conceal ambition; to make the barbarous, unjust, and violent maxims of his rule recognized, respected, and loved, for no prince ever had such great talents, nor better understood the art of governing. Now assuming the fox's skin, now the lion's, no friend was ever so false, no foe of Europe ever so bold. He gave usurpation the appearance of public good; kindled rebellion under pretense of public safety; roused others to drive out royalty and free the nation that he might seize tyranny for himself. He reversed the order of government, and even replaced the laws of religion with others better fitted to his absolute rule. Like all tyrants he was faithless and suspicious, vindictive, bloodthirsty, and a hypocritical demagogue. He abused Parliament, destroyed the upper house, drove out the bishops, overawed the council, and sustained himself only by a powerful army wholly under control.

But Leti was not content with depriving Cromwell of all human virtues. He declared that the Protector was that rare thing in the world, a tyrant without vices, save those of state—ambition and hypocrisy. . . . Such was the character of an English tyrant which did duty for Cromwell's portrait on the Continent for more than a hundred years, and with which Catholic Europe, "seeing in him a scourge and anti-Christ," rested for the most part content.

In England, meanwhile, the new revolution had provided perspective; the rule of Charles II and James II had provided comparison. The generation which had felt his power had passed; and religious feeling as expressed in Dissent, with a conception of the "people" unknown on the Continent, permitted the rise of another school of thought.

One Isaac Kimber, a "General Baptist" minister, . . . reproduced Cromwell's own words; he adduced documents; he enumerated the sources and examples of the Protector's greatness. Above all, he replaced the repulsive effigy of a tyrant with the image of a man among his fellows. He recorded the human traits, the humor, the tenderness, the clemency, the strength and weakness of Cromwell's character, restoring those qualities which, denied by earlier biographers, cut the Protector off from human sympathy.

On the Continent, indeed, this creature of flesh and blood could not compete with Leti's monster, but in England it evoked response. Fifteen years later† John Banks, in a new biography, added two contributions of his own. The one was a defense of the doctrine that a "private man" might hold the sovereignty; the other was a shrewd attack on those who had denied Cromwell the very qualities by which alone he might have risen to eminence. It is absurd, he said, to try "to persuade us that a man without the capacity requisite in a common justice of the peace should be not only too hard for the royal family but even for his own masters and all the ministers and crowned heads with whom he had anything to do." There echoes the doctrine of eighteenth-century common-sense, the logic of Locke, the prophecy of democracy. Yet with it, strangely enough, we come not to the beginning but to the end of an era. For three-quarters of a century after Banks no life of Cromwell of any note appeared, and the four Cromwells—Leti's, Ludlow's, Clarendon's, and Banks'—contended in men's minds for mastery.

Not that men had lost interest in the

----

†1739—Ed.

Protector; on the contrary they were never so busy investigating his character and career. For his fame, as its next adventure, had fallen among a very different kind of folk, the antiquarians. . . . As the climax of this antiquarian school, in the year after the American Revolution, Mark Noble issued his *Memoirs of the Protectoral House of Cromwell.* Wholly uncritical as it was, it did no small service in clearing up that "cloud of distractions rude" by which the real Cromwell had been hidden from the world. . . .

Then, emerging from the antiquarians, his fame suddenly met with another and thus far its greatest adventure. It fell among a new generation of revolutionists. Twice since his death had it been affected by the vicissitudes of politics, both times to its advantage. Now, even while Noble and his patron Shelburne wrote, the American colonies threw off the English yoke; the French people overturned monarchy; the new world and the old were convulsed with war; great popular movements made way in the world; new revolutionary leaders made their appearance on the stage; and for the first time it seemed that an adequate basis of comparison with Cromwell and his times was available. . . .

The era of Napoleon gave fresh impulse to the collection of materials for history. . . . Among the incidental results of Napoleon's career doubtless none would have surprised him more, had he known of it, than his effect on Cromwell's fame. For the first time Europe had felt a tremendous popular convulsion in the French Revolution. The fears of the revolutionary leaders had been more than justified; for they had seen a private man rise to dictatorship. That served in some measure to explain Cromwell to the Continental mind. The parallel was too obvious to be missed and, from the first

year of the Consulate to Waterloo, pamphleteers were busy in pointing it out.

It was too much to expect of the Age of Reform that Godwin should not expound the views of the Republicans. Still less could it be supposed that the most industrious of English literary men-of-all-work, Southey, could restrain his pen. Least of all could it be hoped that he would refrain from pious platitudes. Yet, even so, when summing up the career of "the most fortunate and least flagitious of usurpers" he might have spared quotation from the Litany against heresy and schism and his pious conclusion that "in the world to come—but it is not for us to anticipate the judgments, still less to limit the mercy of the Almighty."

That marks the early Victorian at his worst, and Cromwell, if not the Almighty, would doubtless have felt appropriate gratitude for his biographer's magnanimous restraint. Yet, despite Southey's courteous refusal to influence that final adjudication, it is evident that, under the pressure of the oncoming wave of liberalism, opinion was changing rapidly. It was apparent in the work of the sane and able essayist, John Forster. Though Landor said that Cromwell lived a hypocrite and died a traitor; though Lodge declared that "not even a flowery Whig pen had yet tried to varnish his name with eulogy nor the fierceness of democracy to bedaub with coarse, plain-spoken praise the career of a subtle, treacherous, bloodthirsty, ambitious tyrant;" though Hallam drew his parallel between Cromwell and Napoleon,—Brougham ventured to speak of his administration as brilliant; commended, like Bright, his projects for law reform; and, like Bright and Russell both, adduced his projects for Parliamentary reforms as a model for such action. Finally, Macauley, with his usual acuteness, summed up the case. "No sovereign," he declared, "ever carried to the throne so large a portion of the best qualities of the middling orders, so strong a sympathy with the feelings and interests of his people. He had a high, stout, honest English heart and though his memory has not been taken under the patronage of any part, truth and merit at last prevail." There spoke the voice of triumphing middle-class Liberalism, to Cromwell's virtues very kind, and to his faults a little blind.

The hour and the book were now at hand. Planning for years to write a life of Cromwell, Thomas Carlyle finally, and no doubt wisely, joined the antiquarians—on his own terms—and in 1845 reprinted Cromwell's own words, with Carlylean comment to provide a connected narrative. . . . It was received by nineteenth-century England in the spirit in which Europe received Leti. To Carlyle's generation, which had seen two revolutions and a reform, and which was within three years to experience 1848; which was in a ferment of social, political, intellectual, religious activity; which hoped all things, which believed all things, Carlyle's *Letters and Speeches of Oliver Cromwell* came like the revelation it professed to be. . . . He collected a heap of valuable material in one place. He blew away much of the chaff and dust which had obscured it; he purified the rest; and danced and sang, and shouted and objurgated over the result till the world came to see. Having seen, they believed. This was the service which he rendered to Cromwell's memory. It was a great service and brought reward to both. One may not venture to reckon how many editions his book ran through, nor compute its influence. Carlyle did not, as Acton said, invent Cromwell;

he did not even discover him; but thenceforth the Protector stood forth clear of extraneous matter. Called to the bar of history, his own words won for him the favorable verdict of democracy; . . .the age of rehabilitation was at hand.

One thing remained—to give him an appropriate background and setting in his period. This the earlier biographies, hampered by lack of knowledge and insight, had done imperfectly, if at all. . . . Now, at last, his fame fell among modern historians. Of these the greatest were Professor Gardiner and his coworkers. The first volumes of Gardiner's *History of England from the Accession of James I* appeared in 1863; and, steadily progressing through the next thirty years or more, the patient genius of his scholarship gradually made clear the great secrets of that much-vexed period. Before its revelations the Royalist conception of the brave, bad tyrant gave way, with that of the Republican, and those of their successors.

And what was his conception of Cromwell? "It is mainly this combination of interests—social and religious reform, commerce and empire—," he declares, "which has raised Cromwell to the position of the national hero of the nineteenth century. Like him modern Britain has waged wars, annexed territory, extended trade, and raised her head among the nations. Like him, her sons have been unable to find satisfaction in their achievements unless they could persuade themselves that the general result was beneficial to others besides themselves. . . ."

Here, then, we have the force which made for Cromwell's rehabilitation, the feeling that, for good or ill, he stood somehow for the English people, that he was a symbol of the race from whence he sprang. But there was another force which was of still greater strength. It was the development of popular sovereignty. For, as Professor Gardiner's work went on, England became a democracy, prepared to see in the Cromwellian period the beginnings of that form of government. The effect was immediate and profound. The long search for a formula to explain him seemed at an end. The result was, indeed, no formula, but an appreciation of great underlying forces too long ignored; and Cromwell rose to view no longer the strange, isolated figure of an earlier day, the ambitious, earth-compelling prodigy, but a product of his time, the expression of its spirit, moved often by powers outside himself towards ends which he and his fellows saw dimly if at all.

Once this was grasped, the conclusion was obvious. The work of great scholars from Ranke to Firth contributed to it; and with the concurrent advance of democracy and scholarship the stature of the Protector grew. . . .

Thus, as once none dared to praise him, so, as the tercentenary of his birth approached, no voice save that of Ireland was raised to blame, and that may be, perhaps, some measure of his fame. The old Republican opposition was turned to democratic praise; and Royalist denunciation was as feeble as the royal power, only a few sparks of it remaining to reinforce the long-smouldering Irish hate. . . .

Yet to this, as to all things human, there is an epilogue. . . . We have had hostile Royalist biographies in an age of monarchy; friendly biographies in an age of democracy; should the newest of popular political schools triumph, we shall have again, no doubt, at least a less favorable appreciation from the intellectual heirs of those Levellers and Diggers, whose projects, which seemed so visionary to him, the Protector so unsparingly repressed. For, however heroic the 'un-democratic hero of democracy' has appeared to the democrat, it is too much to hope that we shall not have a new Cromwell from the hand of the Socialist."

The Socialist has already invaded the field of history—and of Cromwell appreciation. To its latest prophet, Mr. Hyndman, the Protector wore another and different guise. To him Cromwell was the representative of the "highly respectable, if sometimes hypocritically ascetic Puritans," the "powerful profiteering class." He had a "curiously complex, crafty and ruthless character, behind" his fanaticism. "He was able to gratify his ambition and determination to be master of them all because, in direct contradiction to what he said of himself, he knew quite early in his career of self-aggrandizement where he was going and how he would get there." He "never at any time had any scruples whatever." "Brutal and merciless," "the thorough representative of the English well-to-do landowning, farming and profiteering class . . . sympathy with democracy and freedom he had none." "From the moment he discovered that none of his possible rivals possessed the politico-warlike qualities that were combined in his person, he threw overboard every opinion and was false to every pledge, that might encumber him in his upward climb."

So, through the revolving years, we come back to Heath again, in twentieth-century dress. But with a difference—we now know the facts, though they beat on Hyndman's intelligence in vain. It may be that this is the last and final adjudication; but if we judge the future by the past, it obviously is not. Only—and this, as Cromwell would have said, is the root of the matter—what possible school of thought is left; what can be the next adventure of his restless fame? . . .

History, like the life it chronicles, has its fashions and its fads. Like life it changes from generation to generation; like those who live that life it alters its point of view and reviews its judgments in accord with its experience and what is known as the spirit of the times. It has not been so long ago that Cromwell was hailed as the "undemocratic hero of democracy." It has not been many years since he was acclaimed as the saviour of liberty. It seems only yesterday that he was pictured as the founder of our modern conceptions of personal freedom in politics as in religion. And what a change have we seen within a decade! If it be true that an interest in his career always portends revolution, the appearance of this new crop of Cromwellian literature may be significant. For Carlyle's hero of liberty has somehow been transformed into Ashley's "conservative dictator." . . . Comparison of Cromwell with Lincoln and Washington has come by some miracle of sea-change into . . . comparison between the Independents and the Nazis, and so, by implication, between Cromwell and Hitler. So the circle has come round full again, from Leti's tyrant without vice through the hero of liberty and democracy to the sad and conservative dictator—though all dictators are of necessity conservative and we have yet to hear of a merry one. For dictatorship, however acquired, is by its very nature never radical, and it is always tragedy, never comedy. Yet, however they differ from each other, all, or nearly all, of these latest evaluations of Cromwell have somewhere concealed within them the concept of dictatorship, whether "unwilling," "reluctant," "melancholy" or "sad" or whatever phrase is used to break the force of that unpleasant phrase which has become too common within the past two decades. The ablest of living publicist-

political philosophers has not hesitated to draw a parallel between the Puritans of seventeenth century England and the Nazis of twentieth century Germany, without, apparently, giving much offence to either side. . . . And it is not without some interest to note that from a German pen has come a study of the "rod of iron" in English affairs, which echoes something of the same spirit.

It is no mere change in terminology which has produced this transformation. It is far deeper than that. It goes to the very root of political action, to the deepest foundations of political existence. The emergence of the word "dictator" from its long seclusion merely reveals another phase in the development of the government of men. It has been long since the phrase "tyrant" was in common use, not as a term of condemnation, as it became a century and a half ago, but as the description of a particular form of administration. It has taken some fifteen hundred years or more for the word "dictator" to be revived, and it has taken incalculable suffering and loss to give it a meaning which it did not originally have. The events of the past twenty years were required to find an appropriate descriptive phrase to fit the position which Cromwell held. For this reason, if for no other, apart from their contents these latest contributions to an appreciation of Cromwell have peculiar interest. They reveal not merely how the world has changed and is changing. They not merely hold the mirror up to the past to see in it the face of the present. They reflect the face of the present in the mirror of the past. It is no mere accident that the past dozen years have seen an extraordinary number of books and articles about Cromwell in German. It is no mere accident that for perhaps the first time there have appeared such contributions in Russian.

It is no mere accident that comparisons have been made between Cromwell, Hitler and Mussolini.

In the same fashion that Napoleon's rise to power helped the people of the continent to understand Cromwell better, so the rise of an Austrian house-painter to the headship of the German Reich, of a newspaper editor-agitator to the leadership of Italy, and of a Georgian bandit to the domination of Russia, have modified our concept of Cromwell's achievement, and perhaps our concept of his place in history. It may well be that, as in the past, another generation may see him in an even different light.

It seems impossible to define once and for all the character of such a man as he was, for before that definition is framed and accepted, some alteration in the spirit and temper and circumstances of the world may alter that concept. . . . But one thing seems certain: such a man contends not only with his own times but with succeeding generations; once he has entered his tomb he has only begun his struggle for his place in history.

Precocious from infancy, THOMAS BABINGTON, LORD MACAULAY (1800–1859) became a main contributor to the *Edinburgh Review* and a member of Parliament. Both in Parliament and in print he was a consummate rhetorician: clear, lucid, and picturesque. He was a prolific reviewer and essayist as well as the author of a celebrated *History of England.* He was unabashedly favorable to those who forwarded Whig principles and took evident delight in passing devastating judgments on their opponents. In this critical review of a Tory historian, he cautioned sternly against the use of simple historical analogies.*

Thomas Babington, Lord Macaulay

Against an Analogy between Napoleon and Cromwell

The death of Charles and the strong measures which led to it raised Cromwell to a height of power fatal to the infant Commonwealth. No men occupy so splendid a place in history as those who have founded monarchies on the ruins of republican institutions. Their glory, if not of the purest, is assuredly of the most seductive and dazzling kind. In nations broken to the curb, in nations long accustomed to be transferred from one tyrant to another, a man without eminent qualities may easily gain supreme power. The defection of a troop of guards, a conspiracy of eunuchs, a popular tumult, might place an indolent senator or a brutal soldier on the throne of the Roman world. Similar revolutions have often occurred in the despotic states of Asia. But a community which has heard the voice of truth and experienced the pleasures of liberty, in which the merits of statesmen and of systems are freely canvassed, in which obedience is paid, not to persons, but to laws, in which magistrates are regarded, not as the lords, but as the servants of the public in which the excitement of a party is a necessary of life, in which political warfare is reduced to a system of tactics; such a community is not easily reduced to servitude. Beasts of burden may easily be managed by a new master. But will the wild ass submit to the bonds? Will the unicorn serve and abide by the crib? Will leviathan hold out his nostrils to the hook? The mythological conqueror of the East, whose enchantments reduced

*From Thomas Babington, Lord Macaulay, *Essays* (London, 1889) pp. 81–85. A review of Hallam's *Constitutional History of England* (London, 1827) reprinted from the *Edinburgh Review,* September, 1828.

wild beasts to the tameness of domestic cattle, and who harnessed lions and tigers to his chariot, is but an imperfect type of those extraordinary minds which have thrown a spell on the fierce spirits of nations unaccustomed to control, and have compelled raging factions to obey their reins and swell their triumph. The enterprise, be it good or bad, is one which requires a truly great man. It demands courage, activity, energy, wisdom, firmness, conspicuous virtues, or vices so splendid and alluring as to resemble virtues.

Those who have succeeded in this arduous undertaking form a very small and a very remarkable class. Parents of tyranny, heirs of freedom, kings among citizens, citizens among kings, they unite in themselves the characteristics of the system which springs from them, and those of the system from which they have sprung. Their reigns shine with a double light, the last and dearest rays of departing freedom mingled with the first and brightest glories of empire in its dawn. The high qualities of such a prince lend to despotism itself a charm drawn from the liberty under which they were formed, and which they have destroyed. He resembles an European who settles within the Tropics, and carries thither the strength and the energetic habits acquired in regions more propitious to the constitution. He differs as widely from princes nursed in the purple of imperial cradles, as the companions of Gama from their dwarfish and imbecile progeny, which, born in a climate unfavourable to its growth and beauty, degenerates more and more, at every descent, from the qualities of the original conquerors.

In this class three men stand preeminent, Caesar, Cromwell, and Bonaparte. The highest place in this remarkable triumvirate belongs undoubtedly to Caesar. He united the talents of Bonaparte to those of Cromwell; and he possessed also, what neither Cromwell nor Bonaparte possessed, learning, taste, wit, eloquence, the sentiments and the manners of an accomplished gentleman.

Between Cromwell and Napoleon Mr Hallam has instituted a parallel, scarcely less ingenious than that which Burke has drawn between Richard Coeur de Lion and Charles the Twelfth of Sweden. In this parallel, however, and indeed throughout his work, we think that he hardly gives Cromwell fair measure. "Cromwell," says he, "far unlike his antitype, never showed any signs of a legislative mind, or any desire to place his renown on that noblest basis, the amelioration of social institutions." The difference in this respect, we conceive, was not in the character of the men, but in the character of the revolutions by means of which they rose to power. The civil war in England had been undertaken to defend and restore; the republicans of France set themselves to destroy. In England, the principles of the common law had never been disturbed, and most even of its forms had been held sacred. In France, the law and its ministers had been swept away together. In France, therefore, legislation necessarily became the first business of the first settled government which rose on the ruins of the old system. The admirers of Inigo Jones have always maintained that his works are inferior to those of Sir Christopher Wren, only because the great fire of London gave Wren such a field for the display of his powers as no architect in the history of the world ever possessed. Similar allowance must be made for Cromwell. If his erected little that was new, it was because there had been no general devastation to clear a space for him. As it was, he reformed the representative system in a most judicious manner. He rendered the administration of justice uniform throughout the island. We will quote a passage from his speech to the Parliament in September, 1656, which contains, we think, simple and rude as the diction is, stronger indications of a legislative mind, than are to be found in the whole range of orations delivered on such occasions before or since.

"There is one general grievance in the nation. It is the law. I think, I may say it, I have as eminent judges in this land as have been had, or that the nation has had for these many years. Truly, I could be particular as to the executive part, to the administration; but that would trouble you. But the truth of it is, there are wicked and abominable laws that will be in your power to alter. To hang a man for sixpence, threepence, I know not what,—to hang for a trifle, and pardon murder, is in the ministration of the law through the ill framing of it. I have known in my experience abominable murders quitted; and to see men lose their lives for petty matters! This is a thing that God will reckon for; and I wish it may not lie upon this nation a day longer than you have an opportunity to give a remedy; and I hope I shall cheerfully join with you in it."

Mr Hallam truly says that, though it is impossible to rank Cromwell with Napoleon as a general, yet "his exploits were as much above the level of his contemporaries, and more the effects of an original uneducated capacity." Bonaparte was trained in the best military schools; the army which he led to Italy was one of the finest that ever existed. Cromwell passed his youth and the prime of his manhood in a civil situation. He never

looked on war till he was more than forty years old. He had first to form himself, and then to form his troops. Out of raw levies he created an army, the bravest and the best disciplined, the most orderly in peace, and the most terrible in war, that Europe had seen. He called this body into existence. He led it to conquest. He never fought a battle without gaining it. He never gained a battle without annihilating the force opposed to him. Yet his victories were not the highest glory of his military system. The respect which his troops paid to property, their attachment to the laws and religion of their country, their submission to the civil power, their temperance, their intelligence, their industry, are without parallel. It was after the Restoration that the spirit which their great leader had infused into them was most signally displayed. At the command of the established government, an established government which had no means of enforcing obedience, fifty thousand soldiers, whose backs no enemy had ever seen, either in domestic or in continental war, laid down their arms, and retired into the mass of the people, thenceforward to be distinguished only by superior diligence, sobriety, and regularity in the pursuits of peace, from the other members of the community which they had saved.

In the general spirit and character of his administration, we think Cromwell far superior to Napoleon. "In civil government," says Mr Hallam, "there can be no adequate parallel between one who had sucked only the dregs of a besotted fanaticism, and one to whom the stores of reason and philosophy were open." These expressions, it seems to us, convey the highest eulogium on our great countryman. Reason and philosophy did not teach the conqueror of Europe to command his passions, or to pursue, as a first object, the happiness of his people. They did not prevent him from risking his fame and his power in a frantic contest against the principles of human nature and the laws of the physical world, against the rage of the winter and the liberty of the sea. They did not exempt him from the influence of that most pernicious of superstitions, a presumptuous fatalism. They did not preserve him from the inebriation of prosperity, or restrain him from indecent querulousness in adversity. On the other hand, the fanaticism of Cromwell never urged him on impracticable undertakings, or confused his perception of the public good. Our countryman, inferior to Bonaparte in invention, was far superior to him in wisdom. The French Emperor is among conquerors what Voltaire is among writers, a miraculous child. His splendid genius was frequently clouded by fits of humour as absurdly perverse as those of the pet of the nursery, who quarrels with his food, and dashes his playthings to pieces. Cromwell was emphatically a man. He possessed, in an eminent degree, that masculine and full-grown robustness of mind, that equally diffused intellectual health, which, if our national partiality does not mislead us, has peculiarly characterised the great men of England. Never was any ruler so conspicuously born for sovereignty. The cup which has intoxicated almost all others sobered him. His spirit, restless from its own buoyancy in a lower sphere, reposed in majestic placidity as soon as it had reached the level congenial to it. He had nothing in common with that large class of men who distinguish themselves in subordinate posts, and whose incapacity becomes obvious as soon as the public voice summons them to take the lead. Rapidly as his fortunes grew, his mind expanded more rapidly still. Insignificant as a private citizen, he was a great general; he was a still greater prince. Napoleon had a theatrical manner, in which the coarseness of a revolutionary guard-room was blended with the ceremony of the old Court of Versailles. Cromwell, by the confession even of his enemies, exhibited in his demeanour the simple and natural nobleness of a man neither ashamed of his origin nor vain of his elevation, of a man who had found his proper place in society, and who felt secure that he was competent to fill it. Easy, even to familiarity, where his own dignity was concerned, he was punctilious only for his country. His own character he left to take care of itself; he left it to be defended by his victories in war, and his reforms in peace. But he was a jealous and implacable guardian of the public honour. He suffered a crazy Quaker to insult him in the gallery of Whitehall, and revenged himself only by liberating him and giving him a dinner. But he was prepared to risk the chances of war to avenge the blood of a private Englishman.

No sovereign ever carried to the throne so large a portion of the best qualities of the middling orders, so strong a sympathy with the feelings and interests of his people. He was sometimes driven to arbitrary measures; but he had a high, stout, honest, English heart. Hence it was that he loved to surround his throne with such men as Hale and Blake. Hence it was that he allowed so large a share of political liberty to his subjects, and that, even when an opposition dangerous to his power and to his person almost compelled him to govern by the sword, he was still anxious to leave a germ from which, at a more favourable season, free institutions might spring. We firmly believe that, if his first Parliament had not commenced its debates by disputing his title, his government would have been as mild at home as it was energetic and able abroad. He was a soldier; he had risen by war. Had his ambition been of an impure or selfish kind, it would have been easy for him to plunge his country into continental hostilities on a large scale, and to dazzle the restless factions which he ruled, by the splendour of his victories. Some of his enemies have sneeringly remarked, that in the successes obtained under his administration he had no personal share; as if a man who had raised himself from obscurity to empire solely by his military talents could have any unworthy reason for shrinking from military enterprise. This reproach is his highest glory. In the success of the English navy he could have no selfish interest. Its triumphs added nothing to his fame; its increase added nothing to his means of overawing his enemies; its great leader was not his friend. Yet he took a peculiar pleasure in encouraging that noble service which, of all the instruments employed by an English government, is the most impotent for mischief, and the most powerful for good. His administration was glorious, but with no vulgar glory. It was not one of those periods of overstrained and convulsive exertion which necessarily produce debility and languor. Its energy was natural, healthful, temperate. He placed England at the head of the Protestant interest, and in the first rank of Christian powers. He taught every nation to value her friendship and to dread her enmity. But he did not squander her resources in a vain attempt to invest her with that supremacy which no power, in the modern system of Europe, can safely affect, or can long retain.

This noble and sober wisdom had its reward. If he did not carry the banners of the Commonwealth in triumph to distant capitals, if he did not adorn White-hall with the spoils of the Stadthouse and the Louvre, if he did not portion out Flanders and Germany into principalities for his kinsmen and his generals, he did not, on the other hand, see his country overrun by the armies of nations which his ambition had provoked. He did not drag out the last years of his life an exile and a prisoner, in an unhealthy climate and under an ungenerous gaoler, raging with the impotent desire of vengeance, and brooding over visions of departed glory. He went down to his grave in the fulness of power and fame; and he left to his son an authority which any man of ordinary firmness and prudence would have retained.

SIR CHARLES FIRTH (1857–1936) spent most of his life at Oxford. After helping the great authority S. R. Gardiner, he inherited Gardiner's mantle as the foremost seventeenth century historian of his generation. Firth was more interested in military and colonial history than his predecessor, and some of this flavor permeates his superb biography of Cromwell. Firth was a copious editor of primary sources, and his *Cromwell* is the work of one thoroughly steeped in the evidence. He attempted an overall assessment of Cromwell's importance and found it to be immense.*

Sir Charles Firth

A High Assessment

Either as a soldier or as a statesman Cromwell was far greater than any Englishman of his time, and he was both soldier and statesman in one. We must look to Caesar or Napoleon to find a parallel for this union of high political and military ability in one man. Cromwell was not as great a man as Caesar or Napoleon, and he played his part on a smaller stage, but he "bestrode the narrow world" of Puritan England "like a colossus."

As a soldier he not only won great victories, but created the instrument with which he won them. Out of the military chaos which existed when the war began he organised the force which made Puritanism victorious. The New Model and the armies of the Republic and the Protectorate were but his regiment of Ironsides on a larger scale. As in that regiment, the officers were carefully chosen. If possible, they were gentlemen; if gentlemen could not be had, plain yeomen or citizens; in any case, "men patient of wants, faithful and conscientious in their employment." Character as well as military skill was requisite. A colonel once complained that a captain whom Cromwell had appointed to his regiment was a better preacher than fighter. "Truly," answered Cromwell, "I think that he that prays and preaches best will fight best. I know nothing that will give the like courage and confidence as the knowledge of God in Christ will. I assure you he is a good man and a good officer." Inefficiency, on the other hand,

*From Sir Charles H. Firth, *Oliver Cromwell and the Rule of the Puritans in England* (London, 1938) pp. 467–486. Used by permission of the publishers, Oxford University Press, London, E.C. 4.

certain heresies which were regarded as particularly blasphemous, and moral backslidings in general, led at once to the cashiering of any officer found guilty of them.

Officers, it has been well said, are the soul of an army; and the efficiency and good conduct which Cromwell required of his, they exacted from the rank and file. Most of the private soldiers were volunteers, though there were many pressed men amongst them, and it cannot be said that all those who fought for Puritanism were saints in any sense of the word. But regular pay and severe discipline made them in peace the best conducted soldiers in Europe, and in war an army "who could go anywhere and do anything." A common spirit bound men and officers together. It was their pride that they were not a mere mercenary army, but men who fought for principles as well as for pay. Cromwell succeeded in inspiring them not only with implicit confidence in his leadership, but with something of his own high enthusiasm. He had the power of influencing masses of men which Napoleon possessed. So he made an army on which, as Clarendon said, "victory seemed entailed"—"an army whose order and discipline, whose sobriety and manners, whose courage and success, made it famous and terrible over the world."

Cromwell's victories, however, were due to his own military genius even more than to the quality of his troops. The most remarkable thing in his military career is that it began so late. Most successful generals have been trained to arms from their youth, but Cromwell was forty-three years old before he heard a shot fired or set a squadron in the field. How was it, people often ask, that an untrained country gentleman beat soldiers who had learnt their trade under the most famous captains in Europe? The answer is that Cromwell had a natural aptitude for war, and that circumstances were singularly favourable to its rapid and full development. At the outset of the war he showed an energy, a resolution, and a judgment which proved his possession of those qualities of intellect and character which war demands of leaders. The peculiar nature of the war, the absence of any general direction, and the disorganisation of the parliamentary forces gave him free scope for the exercise of these qualities. In the early part of the war each local leader fought for his own hand, and conducted a little campaign of his own. Subordinate officers possessed a freedom of action which subordinates rarely get, and with independence and responsibility good men ripened fast. At first, Cromwell was matched against opponents as untrained as himself, till by constant fighting he learnt how to fight. In a happy phrase Marvell speaks of Cromwell's "industrious valour." If he learnt the lessons of war quicker than other men it was because he concentrated all his faculties on the task, let no opportunity slip, and made every experience fruitful.

It was as a leader of cavalry that Cromwell earned his first laurels. In attack he was sudden and irresistibly vigorous. Like Rupert he loved to head his charging troopers himself, but in the heat of battle he controlled them with a firmer hand. When the enemy immediately opposed to him was broken he turned a vigilant eye on the battle, ready to throw his victorious squadrons into the scale, either to redress the balance or to complete the victory. At Marston Moor, as on many another field, he proved that he possessed that faculty of coming to a prompt and sure conclusion in sudden emergencies which Napier terms "the sure mark of a master spirit in war." When the fate of the battle was once decided he launched forth his swordsmen in swift and unsparing pursuit. "We had the execution of them two or three miles" is the grim phrase in which he describes the conclusion of his fight at Grantham, and after Naseby Cromwell's cavalry pursued for twelve miles.

When he rose to command an army, Cromwell's management of it in battle was marked by the same characteristics as his handling of his division of cavalry. In the early battles of the Civil War there was a strong family likeness: there was an absence of any generalship on either side. The general-in-chief exhibited his skill by his method of drawing up his army and his choice of a position; but when the battle began the army seemed to slip from his control. Each commander of a division acted independently; there was little co-operation between the different parts of the army; there was no sign of a directing brain. Cromwell, on the other hand, directed the movements of his army with the same purposeful energy with which he controlled his troopers. Its different divisions had each their definite task assigned to them, and their movements were so combined that each played its part in carrying out the general plan. The best example of Cromwell's tactical skill is the battle of Dunbar. There, though far inferior in numbers, Cromwell held in check half the enemy's army with his artillery and a fraction of his forces, while he attacked with all his strength the key of the enemy's position, and decided the fate of the day by bringing a strong reserve into action at the crisis of the battle. Whenever the victory was gained it was utilised to the utmost. At Dunbar the Scots lost thirteen thousand men out of twenty-two thousand; after Preston less than a third of

Hamilton's army succeeded in effecting their return to Scotland: after Worcester, not one troop or one company made good its retreat.

Cromwell's strategy, compared with that of contemporary generals, was remarkable for boldness and vigour. It reflected the energy of his character, but it was originally dictated by political as well as military considerations. . . . Instead of imitating the cautious defensive system popular with professional soldiers, he adopted a system which promised more decisive results. "Cromwell," says a military critic, "was the first great exponent of the modern method of war. His was the strategy of Napoleon and Von Moltke, the strategy which, neglecting fortresses and the means of artificial defence as of secondary importance, strikes first at the army in the field." . . .

[Yet] Cromwell could adapt his strategy with unfailing success to the conditions of the theatre in which he waged war and to the character of the antagonists he had to meet. His military genius was equal to every duty which fate imposed upon him.

Experts alone can determine Cromwell's precise place amongst great generals. Cromwell himself would have held it the highest honour to be classed with Gustavus Adolphus either as soldier or statesman. Each was the organiser of the army he led to victory, each an innovator in war—Gustavus in tactics, Cromwell in strategy. Gustavus was the champion of European Protestantism as Oliver wished to be, and each while fighting for his creed contrived to further also the material interests of his country. But whatever similarity existed between their aims the position of an hereditary monarch and an usurper are too different for the parallel to be a complete one. On the other hand, the familiar comparison of Cromwell with Napoleon is justified rather by the remembrance between their careers than by any likeness between their characters. Each was the child of a revolution, brought by military success to the front rank, and raised by his own act to the highest. Each, after domestic convulsions, laboured to rebuild the fabric of civil government, and to found the State on a new basis. But the revolutions which raised them to power were of a different nature and demanded different qualities in the two rulers. . . .

In one of his speeches Cromwell states in very explicit language the rule which he followed in his public life. "I have been called to several employments in this nation, and I did endeavour to discharge the duty of an honest man to God and His people's interest, and to this Commonwealth."

What did these phrases mean? If anyone had asked Cromwell what his duty to God was in public affairs, he would have answered that it was to do God's will. "We all desire," he said to his brother officers in 1647, "to lay this as the foundation of all our actions, to do that which is the will of God." He urged them to deliberate well before acting, "that we may see that the things we do have the will of God in them." For to act inconsiderately was to incur the risk of acting counter to God's design, and so "to be found fighting against God."

But, in the maze of English politics, how were men to ascertain what that will was? Some Puritans claimed to have had it directly revealed to them, and put forward their personal convictions as the dictates of Heaven. Cromwell never did so. "I cannot say," he declared in a prayer-meeting where such revelations had been alleged, "that I have received anything that I can speak as in the name of the Lord." He believed that men might

still "be spoken unto by the Spirit of God," but when these "divine impressions and divine discoveries" were made arguments for political action, they must be received with the greatest caution. For the danger of self-deception was very real. "We are very apt, all of us," said he, "to call that Faith, that perhaps may be but carnal imagination." Once he warned the Scottish clergy that there was "a carnal confidence upon misunderstood and misapplied precepts" which might be termed "spiritual drunkenness."

For his own part, Cromwell believed in "dispensations" rather than "revelations." Since all things which happened in the world were determined by God's will, the statesman's problem was to discover the hidden purpose which underlay events. When he announced his victory at Preston he bade Parliament enquire "what the mind of God is in all that and what our duty is." "Seek to know what the mind of God is in all that chain of Providence," was his counsel to his doubting friend, Colonel Hammond. With Cromwell, in every political crisis this attempt to interpret the meaning of events was part of the mental process which preceded action. As it was difficult to be sure what that meaning was, he was often slow to make up his mind, preferring to watch events a little longer and to allow them to develop in order to get more light. This slowness was not the result of indecision, but a deliberate suspension of judgment. When his mind was made up there was no hesitation, no looking back; he struck with the same energy in politics as in war.

This system of being guided by events had its dangers. Political inconsistency is generally attributed to dishonesty, and Cromwell's inconsistency was open and palpable. One year he was foremost in pressing for an agreement with the

King, another foremost in bringing him to the block; now all for a republic, now all for a government with some element of monarchy in it. His changes of policy were so sudden that even friends found it difficult to excuse them. A pamphleteer, who believed in the honesty of Cromwell's motives, lamented his "sudden engaging for and sudden turning from things," as arguing inconstancy and want of foresight. Moreover the effect of this inconsistency was aggravated by the violent zeal with which Cromwell threw himself into the execution of each new policy. It was part of his nature, like "the exceedingly fiery temper" mentioned by his steward. "I am often taken," said Cromwell in 1647, "for one that goes too fast," adding that men of such a kind were disposed to think the dangers in their way rather imaginary than real, and sometimes to make more haste than good speed. This piece of self-criticism was just, and it explains some of his mistakes. The forcible dissolution of the Long Parliament in 1653 would never have taken place if Cromwell had fully appreciated the dangers which it would bring upon the Puritan cause.

On the other hand, this failure to look far enough ahead, while it detracts from Cromwell's statesmanship, helps to vindicate his integrity. He was too much taken up with the necessities of the present to devise a deep-laid scheme for making himself great. He told the French Ambassador in 1647, with a sort of surprise, that a man never rose so high as when he did not know where he was going. To his Parliaments he spoke of himself as having seen nothing in God's dispensations long beforehand. "These issues and events," he said in 1656, "have not been forecast, but were sudden providences in things." By this series of unforeseen events, necessitating first one

step on his part and then the next, he had been raised to the post of Protector. "I did out of necessity undertake that business," said he, "which place I undertook, not so much out of a hope of doing any good, as out of a desire to prevent mischief and evil which I did see was imminent in the nation."

Conscious, therefore, that he had not plotted to bring about his own elevation, Cromwell resented nothing so much as the charge that he had "made the necessities" to which it was due. For it was not merely an imputation on his own honesty, but a kind of atheism, as if the world was governed by the craft of men, not by the wisdom of God. People said, "It was the cunning of my Lord Protector that hath brought it about," when in reality these great revolutions were "God's revolutions." "Whatsoever you may judge men for, however you may say this is cunning, and politic, and subtle, take heed how you judge His revolutions as the product of men's invention."

Cromwell said this with perfect sincerity. He felt that he was but a blind instrument in the hands of a higher power. Yet he had shaped the issue of events with such power and had imposed his interpretation of their meaning upon them with such decision, that neither contemporaries nor historians could limit to so little the sphere of his free will.

It was possible to "make too much of outward dispensations," and Cromwell owned that perhaps he did so. His system of being guided by events instead of revelations did not put an end to the possibility of self-deception, though it made it less likely. "Men," as Shakespeare says, "may construe things after their fashion clean from the purpose of the things themselves." But if Cromwell sometimes mistook the meaning of facts he never failed to realise their importance. "If the fact be so," he once said, "why should we sport with it?" and the saying is a characteristic one. He was therefore more practical and less visionary than other statesmen of his party; more open-minded and better able to adapt his policy to the changing circumstances and changing needs of the times. To many contemporary politicians, the exact carrying out of some cut-and-dried political programme seemed the height of political wisdom. The Levellers with their Agreement of the People and the Scottish Presbyterians with their Covenant are typical examples. The persistent adhesion of the Covenanters to their old formulas, in spite of defeats and altered conditions, Cromwell regarded as blindness to the teaching of events. They were blind to God's great dispensations, he told the Scottish ministers, out of mere wilfulness, "because the things did not work forth their platform, and the great God did not come down to their minds and thoughts." He would have felt himself guilty of the same fault if he had obstinately adhered either to a republic or a monarchy under all circumstances. Forms of government were neither good nor bad in themselves. Either form might be good: it depended on the condition of England at the moment, on the temper of the people, on the question which was more compatible with the welfare of the Cause, which more answerable to God's purpose as revealed in events. It was reported that Cromwell had said that it was lawful to pass through all forms to accomplish his ends, and if "forms" be taken to mean forms of government, and "ends" political aims, there can be no doubt that he thought so. However much he varied his means, his ends remained the same.

To understand what Cromwell's political aims were, it is necessary to enquire what he meant when he spoke of his discharging his duty to "the interest of the people of God and this Commonwealth." The order in which he places them is in itself significant. First, he put the duty to a section of the English people; last, the duty to the English people in general. Cromwell was full of patriotic pride. Once, when he was enumerating to Parliament the dangers which threatened the State, he wound up by saying that the enumeration should cause no despondency, "as truly I think it will not; for we are Englishmen: that is one good fact." "The English," he said on another occasion, "are a people that have been like other nations, sometimes up and sometimes down in our honour in the world, but never yet so low but we might measure with other nations." Several times in his speeches he termed the English "the best people in the world." Best, because "having the highest and clearest profession amongst them of the greatest glory—namely, religion." Best, because in the midst of the English people there was as it were another people, "a people that are to God as the apple of His eye," "His peculiar interest" "the people of God." "When I say the people of God," he explained, "I mean the large comprehension of them under the several forms of godliness in this nation"; or, in other words, all sects of Puritans.

To Cromwell the interest of the people of God and the interest of the nation were two distinct things, but he did not think them irreconcilable. "He sings sweetly," said Cromwell, "that sings a song of reconciliation between these two interests, and it is a pitiful fancy to think they are inconsistent." At the same time the liberty of the people of God was more important than the civil liberty and interest of the nation, "which is and ought to be subordinate to the more peculiar interest of God, yet is the next best God hath given men in this world." Religious freedom was more important than political freedom. Cromwell emphatically condemned the politicians who said, "If we could but exercise wisdom to gain civil liberty, religion would follow." Such men were "men of a hesitating spirit," and "under the bondage of scruples." They were little better than the carnal men who cared for none of these things. They could never "rise to such a spiritual heat" as the Cause demanded. Yet the truth was that half the Republican party and an overwhelming majority of the English people held the view which he condemned.

Cromwell wished to govern constitutionally. No theory of the divine right of an able man to govern the incapable multitude blinded his eyes to the fact that self-government was the inheritance and right of the English people. He accepted in the main the first principle of democracy, the doctrine of the sovereignty of the people, or, as he phrased it, "that the foundation of supremacy is in the people and to be by them set down in their representatives." More than once he declared that the good of the governed was the supreme end of all governments, and he claimed that his own government acted "for the good of the people, and for their interest, and without respect had to any other interest." But government for the people did not necessarily mean government by the people. "That's the question," said Cromwell, "what's for their good, not what pleases them," and the history of the Protectorate was a commentary on this text. Some stable government was necessary to prevent either a return to anarchy or the restoration of the Stuarts. Therefore he was determined to maintain his own government, with the assistance of

Parliament if possible, without it if he must. If it became necessary to suspend for a time the liberties of the subject or to levy taxes without parliamentary sanction, he was prepared to do it. In the end the English people would recognise that he had acted for their good. "Ask them," said he, "whether they would prefer the having of their will, though it be their destruction, rather than comply with things of necessity?" He felt confident the answer would be in his favour.

England might have acquiesced in this temporary dictatorship in the hope of a gradual return to constitutional government. What it could not accept was the permanent limitation of the sovereignty of the people in the interest of the Puritan minority whom Cromwell termed the people of God. Yet it was at this object that all the constitutional settlements of the Protectorate aimed. It was in the interest of this minority that the Instrument of Government restricted the power of Parliament and made the Protector the guardian of the constitution. It was in their interest that the Petition and Advice re-established a House of Lords. . . .

Cromwell trusted that the real benefits his government conferred would reconcile the majority of the nation to the rule of the minority and "win the people to the interest of Jesus Christ." Thus the long hostility between the people and "the people of God" would end at last in reconciliation.

It was a fallacious hope. Puritanism was spending its strength in the vain endeavour to make England Puritan by force. The enthusiasm which had undertaken to transform the world was being conformed to it. A change was coming over the party which supported the Protector; it had lost many of the "men of conscience;" it had attracted many of the time-servers and camp-followers of politics; it was ceasing to be a party held together by religious interests, and becoming a coalition held together by material interests and political necessities. Cromwell once rebuked the Scottish clergy for "meddling with worldly policies and mixtures of worldly power" to set up that which they called "the kingdom of Christ," and warned them that "the Sion promised" would not be built "with such untempered mortar." He had fallen into the same error himself, and the rule of Puritanism was founded on shifting sands. So the Protector's institutions perished with him and his work ended in apparent failure. Yet he had achieved great things. Thanks to his sword absolute monarchy failed to take root in English soil. Thanks to his sword Great Britain emerged from the chaos of the civil wars one strong state instead of three separate and hostile communities. Nor were the results of his action entirely negative. The ideas which inspired his policy exerted a lasting influence on the development of the English state. Thirty years after his death the religious liberty for which he fought was established by law. The union with Scotland and Ireland, which the Statesmen of the Restoration undid, the statesmen of the eighteenth century effected. The mastery of the seas he had desired to gain, and the Greater Britain he had sought to build up became sober realities. Thus others perfected the work which he had designed and attempted.

Cromwell remained throughout his life too much the champion of a party to be accepted as a national hero by later generations, but in serving his Cause he served his country too. No English ruler did more to shape the future of the land he governed, none showed more clearly in his acts the "plain heroic magnitude of mind."

JOHN, VISCOUNT MORLEY (1838–1923) turned his back on holy orders for a career in writing and editing. He moved among radical literary groups and imbibed their mid-Victorian individualism. After winning a seat in the House of Commons in 1883, he threw his support to Gladstone on the Irish question. Like Gladstone, Morley opposed cavalier imperial expansionism. On the eve of the First World War, Morley resigned in protest against the imminent declaration of war. At the end he leaned somewhat toward socialism, but he remained essentially a liberal individualist all his life. His long and arduous political career gave a certain depth of experience to his historical biographies, including studies of Cobden, Gladstone, and Cromwell. Posterity may remember him less as a statesman than as a perceptive essayist and biographer.*

John Morley

Political Ends Miscarry

To imply that Cromwell stands in the line of European dictators with Charles V or Louis XIV or Napoleon is a hyperbole that does him both less than justice and more. Guizot brings us nearer to the truth when he counts Cromwell, William III, and Washington as chiefs and representatives of sovereign crises that have settled the destinies of nations. When we go on to ask what precisely was Cromwell's share in a mission so supreme, the answer, if we seek it away from the prepossessions of modern controversy, is not hard to discern. It was by his military genius, by the might of the legions that he created and controlled and led to victory upon victory; it was at Marston and Naseby, at Preston and Worcester, in Ireland and at Dunbar, that Cromwell set his deep mark on the destinies of England as she was, and of that vaster dominion into which the English realm was in the course of ages to be transformed. He was chief of a party who shared his own strong perception that neither civil freedom nor political could be made secure without the sword, and happily the swordsman showed himself consummate. In speed and vigour, in dash and in prudence, in force of shock and quick steadiness of recovery; in sieges, marches, long wasting campaigns, pitched engagements; as commander of horse, as tactician, and as strategist, the modern expert ranks Cromwell among the foremost masters of the rough art of war in every branch. Above all, he created the instrument which in discipline, skill, and those highest mili-

*From John Morley, *Oliver Cromwell: The Works of John Morley,* 15 vols. (London, 1921) V, 428–435. Used by permission of the publishers, Macmillan and Co., London, W.C. 2.

tary virtues that come of moral virtues, has never been surpassed.

In our own half-century now closing, alike in Western Europe and across the Atlantic, the torch of war has been lighted rather for Unity of race or state, than for Liberty. Cromwell struck for both. It was his armed right hand that crushed the absolutist pretensions alike of crown and mitre, and then forced the three kingdoms into the mould of a single state. It was at those decisive moments when the trembling balance hung on fortune in the battlefield, that the unconquerable captain turned the scale. After we have discussed all the minor aspects of his special policies on this occasion or the other, after we have scanned all the secondary features of his rule, this is still what in a single sentence defines the true place of Cromwell in our history.

Along with that paramount claim, he performed the service of keeping a provisional form of peace, and delivering the nation from the anarchy in which both order and freedom would have been submerged. He made what some of the best of his contemporaries thought dire mistakes; he forsook many principles in his choice of means, which he intended to preserve in working out the end; and many of his difficulties were of his own creation. Yet watchfulness, self-effacement, versatility, and resource, for the time and on the surface repaired all, and as "constable of the parish" his persistency was unfaltering and unmatched. In the harder task of laying the foundations of a deeper order that might be expected to stand after his own imperious control should be withdrawn, he was beaten. He hardly counted on more. In words already quoted, "I did out of necessity," he said, "undertake that business, not so much out of a hope of doing any good, as out of a desire to prevent mischief and evil."

He reared no dam nor bulwark strong enough to coerce either the floods of revolutionary faction or the reactionary tides that came after. "Does not your peace," as Henry Cromwell asked, "depend upon his Highness' life, and upon his peculiar skill and faculty and personal interest in the army?" That is to say, the Protectorate was no system, but only the transitory expedient of individual supremacy. . . .

It is hard to resist the view that Cromwell's revolution was the end of the mediaeval, rather than the beginning of the modern era. He certainly had little of the faith in progress that became the inspiration of a later age. His respect for Public Opinion—supposed to be the driving force of modern government—was a strictly limited regard. In one sense he was no democrat, for he declared, as we have seen, that the question is not what pleases people, but what is for their good. This came rather near to Charles's words as he stood upon the scaffold, that the people's liberty lay in the laws, "not their having a share in government; that is nothing pertaining to them." But then, on the other hand, Cromwell was equally strong that things obtained by force, though never so good in themselves, are both less to the ruler's honour and less likely to last. "What we gain in a free way, it is better than twice as much in a forced, and will be more truly ours and our posterity's" (*ante*, p. 202); and the safest test of any constitution is its acceptance by the people. And again, "It will be found an unjust and unwise jealousy to deprive a man of his natural liberty upon a supposition he may abuse it." The root of all external freedom is here.

In saying that Cromwell had the spirit, insight, and grasp that fit a man to wield power in high affairs, we only repeat that he had the instinct of government, and this is a very different thing from either a taste for abstract ideas of politics, or the passion for liberty. The instinct of order has been so often the gift of a tyrant as of a hero, as common to some of the worst hearts in human history as to some of the best. Cromwell was no Frederick the Great, who spoke of mankind as *diese verdammte Rasse,* that accursed tribe. He belonged to the rarer and nobler type of governing men, who see the golden side, who count faith, pity, hope among the counsels of practical wisdom, and who for political power seek a moral base. This is a key to men's admiration for him. His ideals were high, his fidelity to them, though sometimes clouded, as still abiding, his ambition was pure. Yet it can hardly be accident that has turned him into one of the idols of the school who hold, shyly as yet in England, but nakedly in Germany, that might is a token of right, and that the strength and power of the state is an end that at once tests and justifies all means.

When it is claimed that no English ruler did more than Cromwell to shape the future of the land he governed, we run some risk of straining history only to procure incense for retrograde ideals. Many would contend that Thomas Cromwell, in deciding the future of one of the most powerful standing institutions of the country, exercised a profounder influence than Oliver. Then, if Cromwell did little to shape the future of the church of England, neither did he shape the future of the parliament of England. On the side of constitutional construction, unwelcome as it may sound, a more important place belongs to the sage and steadfast, though rather unheroic Walpole. The development of the England constitution has in truth proceeded on lines that Cromwell profoundly disliked. The idea of a parliament always sitting and actively re-

viewing the details of administration was in his sight an intolerable mischief. It was almost the only system against which his supple mind, so indifferent as it was to all constitutional forms, stood inflexible. Yet this, for good or ill, is our system to-day, and the system of the wide host of political communities that have followed our parliamentary model. When it is said again, that it was owing to Cromwell that Nonconformity had time to take such deep root as to defy the storm of the Restoration, do we not overlook the original strength of all those giant puritan fibres from which both the Rebellion and Cromwell himself had sprung? It was not a man, not even such a man as Oliver, it was the same underlying spiritual forces that made the Rebellion, which also held fast against the Restoration. It would hardly be more forced to say that Cromwell was the founder of Nonconformity.

It has been called a common error of our day to ascribe far too much to the designs and the influence of eminent men, of rulers, and of governments. The reproach is just and should impress us. The momentum of past events; the spontaneous impulses of the mass of a nation or a race; the pressure of general hopes and fears; the new things learned in the onward and diversified motions of "the great spirit of human knowledge"—all these have more to do with the progress of the world's affairs than the deliberate views of even the most determined and far-sighted of its individual leaders. Thirty years after the death of the Protector, a more successful revolution came about. The law was made more just, the tribunals were purified, the rights of conscience received at least a partial recognition, the press began to enjoy a freedom for which Milton had made a glorious appeal, but which Cromwell never dared concede. Yet the Declaration of Right and the

Toleration Act issued from a stream of ideas and maxims, aims and methods that were not puritan. New tributaries had already swollen the volume and changed the currents of that broad confluence of manners, morals, government, belief, of whose breast Time guides the voyages of mankind. The age of Rationalism with its bright lights and sobering shadows had begun. Some ninety years after 1688, another revolution followed in the England across the Atlantic, and the gulf between Cromwell and Jefferson is measure of the vast distance the minds of men had travelled. With the death of Cromwell, though the free churches remained as nurseries of strong-hearted civil feeling, the brief life of puritan theocracy in England expired. It was a phase of a movement that left an inheritance of many noble thoughts, the memory of a brave struggle for human freedom, and a procession of strenuous master-spirits with Milton and Cromwell at their head. Political ends miscarry, and the revolutionary leader treads a path of fire. True wisdom is to learn how we may combine sane verdicts on the historic event, with a just estimation in the actor of those qualities of high endeavour on which, amid incessant change of formula, direction, fashion, and ideal, the world's best hopes in every age depend.

Although his interests range from early Christian history to Hitler, H. R. TREVOR-ROPER (1916–) is expert in the seventeenth century. From his chair as Regius Professor of Modern History at Oxford, he has hurled thunderbolts at other celebrated historians such as Arnold Toynbee, A. J. P. Taylor, and E. H. Carr. His reviews and essays have done much to make history one of the liveliest of humane disciplines. He is a non-doctrinaire conservative who can praise Macaulay and blame Hume, and he does not hesitate to seek the social causes of the English Revolution—albeit un-Marxian causes. His most stimulating ideas have been thrust forward in controversies. The exchanges with the late Professor Tawney and Lawrence Stone (now at Princeton) on the condition of the aristocracy and gentry prior to the Civil War have become classics of their kind. His flair for controversy shows in this bebunking of Cromwell. But is it fair?*

H. R. Trevor-Roper

Cromwell's Failure with Parliaments

Oliver Cromwell and his parliaments—the theme is almost a tragi-comedy. Cromwell was himself a member of parliament; he was the appointed general of the armies of parliament; and the Victorians, in the greatest days of parliamentary government, set up his statue outside the rebuilt Houses of Parliament. But what were Cromwell's relations with parliament? The Long Parliament, which appointed him, he first purged by force and then violently expelled from authority. His own parliament, the Parliament of Saints, which to a large extent was nominated by his government, was carried away by hysteria, rent by intrigue, and dissolved, after six months, by an undignified act of suicide. Of the parliaments of the Protectorate, elected on a new franchise and within new limits determined by the government, the first was purged by force within a week and dissolved, by a trick hardly distinguishable from fraud, before its legal term; the second was purged by fraud at the beginning and, when that fraud was reversed, became at once unmanageable and was dissolved within a fortnight. On a superficial view, Cromwell was as great an enemy of parliament as ever Charles I or Archbishop Laud had been, the only difference being that, as an enemy, he

*From H. R. Trevor-Roper, "Oliver Cromwell and His Parliaments," in *Essays Presented to Sir Lewis Namier,* eds. Richard Parcs and A. J. P. Taylor (London, 1956) pp. 1–48. Used by permission of the author and the publishers, Macmillan and Co., London, W. C. 2, and St. Martin's Press, New York, 10.

was more successful: he scattered all his parliaments and died in his bed, while theirs deprived them of their power and brought them both ultimately to the block. . . .

Why was Oliver Cromwell so uniformly unsuccessful with his parliaments? To answer this question we must first look a little more closely at the aims and character both of Oliver Cromwell and of that opposition to the court of Charles I of which he was first an obscure and ultimately the most powerful representative: an opposition not of practised politicians (the practised politicians of 1640 were dead, or had lost control by 1644) nor of City Merchants (the great London merchants were largely royalist in 1640), but of gentry: the backwoods gentry who, in 1640, sat on the back benches† of parliament, but who, as war and revolution progressed, gradually broke through the crumbling leadership which had at first contained them: the 'Independents'.

Now these 'Independent' gentry, it is important to emphasize, were not, as a class, revolutionary: that is, they did not hold revolutionary ideas. There were revolutionaries among the Independents, of course. There were revolutionaries in parliament, men like 'Harry Marten and his gang'—Henry Neville, Thomas Chaloner and others: intellectual republicans who had travelled in Italy, read Machiavelli and Botero, and cultivated the doctrine of raison d'état; just as there were also revolutionaries outside parliament: the Levellers and the Fifth Monarchy Men. But if these men were the successive sparks which kindled the various stages of revolution, they were not the essential tinder of it. The majority of the members of parliament, who at first accidentally

† Members who were not important enough to occupy seats near or on the front benches that face each other across the Hall.—Ed.

launched the revolutionary movement and were afterwards borne along or consumed by it, were not clear-headed men like these. They were not thinkers or even dreamers, but plain, conservative, untravelled country-gentlemen whose passion came not from radical thought or systematic doctrine but from indignation: indignation which the electioneering ability of a few great lords and the parliamentary genius of John Pym had contrived to turn into a political force, and which no later leaders were able wholly either to harness or to contain. These were the men who formed the solid stuff of parliamentary opposition to Charles I: men whose social views were conservative enough, but whose political passions were radical, and became more radical as they discovered depth below depth of royal duplicity. These were the men who became, in time, the 'Independents'; and Cromwell, though he transcended them in personality and military genius, was their typical, if also their greatest, representative. . . .

And what were the positive ideals of these outraged but largely unpolitical conservative gentry? Naturally, in the circumstances, they were not very constructive. These men looked back, not forward; back from the House of Stuart which had so insulted them to the House of Tudor of which their fathers had spoken, and in the reign of Elizabeth they discovered, or invented, a golden age: an age when the court had been, as it seemed, in harmony with the country and the Crown with its parliaments; an age when a Protestant queen, governing parsimoniously at home and laying only tolerable burdens on 'her faithful Commons', had nevertheless made England glorious abroad—head of 'the Protestant Interest' throughout the world, victor over Spain in the Indies, protector of the Netherlands in Europe. Since 1603 that glorious position had been lost. King James had alienated the gentry, abandoned Protestantism for Arminian policy at home and popish alliances abroad, made peace with Spain, and surrendered, with the 'cautionary towns', the protectorate over the Netherlands. When the religious struggle had broken out anew in Europe, it was not the king of England who had inherited the mantle of Queen Elizabeth as defender of the Protestant faith: it was a new champion from the North, the king of Sweden. In the 1630's when Gustavus Adolphus swept triumphantly through Germany, he became the hero of the frustrated, mutinous English gentry; and when he fell at Lützen, scarcely an English squire but wrote, in his manor-house a doggerel epitaph on the new pole-star of his loyalty, 'the Lion of the North'.

Such were the basic political views, or prejudices, of the English back-benchers who poured into parliament in 1640. But they had social views also, and these too led them back to the same golden age of the Protestant queen. First there was the desire for decentralization—the revolt of the provinces and of the provincial gentry not only against the growing, parasitic Stuart court but also against the growing, 'dropsical' City of London, against the centralized Church, whether Anglican or presbyterian, and against the expensive monopoly of higher education by the two great universities. All this was implied in the independent programme. And also, what we must never forget, for it was a great element in the Protestant tradition, there was the demand for an organic society responsible for the welfare of its members. Ever since, among the first Reformers, 'the Commonwealth Men' had protested against the irresponsibility, the practical inhumanity,

the privileged uselessness of the pre-Reformation Church, the English Protestants had laid emphasis upon the collective nature of society and the mutual obligations of the classes which make it up. Under Elizabeth, and especially in the long reign of Lord Burghley, something more than lip-service had been paid to this ideal; but under the Stuarts, and particularly in the reign of James I (that formative era of English puritanism), the ideal had again been eclipsed as court and Church became once again openly parasitic upon society. Those were the years in which the cry for social justice had become insistent and the Common Law, so extolled by its most successful practitioner, Sir Edward Coke, became, in other eyes, one of the most oppressive of social burdens. When the Anglican Archbishop Laud had failed in his desperate, purblind but in some respects heroic efforts to reform society centrally and from above, the puritan Opposition inherited much of his programme and sought to realize it in another form, as a decentralized, 'Independent' commonwealth. The radicals would have achieved such reformation violently and devised new paper constitutions to achieve and preserve it. The conservative puritans, who were radical only in temper, not in their social or political doctrines, shied away from such novel remedies. Believing just as sincerely in a better, more decentralized, more responsible society, they looked for its achievement not to Utopia or Oceana but, once again, to a revived Elizabethan age. . . .

None of them dreamed, in 1640, of revolution, either in Church or in State. They were neither separatists nor republicans. What they wanted was a king who, unlike Charles I, but like the Queen Elizabeth of their imagination, would work the existing institutions in the good old sense; bishops who, unlike the Laudian bishops . . . would supervise their flocks in the good old sense! . . . It was only by an extraordinary and quite unpredictable turn of events that one of these back-benchers, Oliver Cromwell, having ruined all existing institutions, found himself, in 1649, faced with the responsibility of achieving, or restoring, the lost balance of society. . . .

Cromwell was not a radical or an intellectual or a young man. He did not want to continue the revolution, which had already, in his eyes and in the eyes of his fellow-gentry, got out of control. He wanted to stop it, to bring it under control, to bring 'settlement' after an unfortunate but, as it had turned out, unavoidable period of 'blood and confusion'. Nor did he believe in new constitutions, or indeed in any constitutions at all. . . .

Opportunists who do not believe in the necessity of particular constitutions take what lies nearest to hand, and what lay nearest to Cromwell's hand when he found himself called upon to restore his ideal Elizabethan society was naturally the surviving débris of the Elizabethan constitution. Parliament had been savaged—and by none more than himself—but its rump was there; the king had been destroyed, but he himself stood, if somewhat incongruously, in his place. Naturally he saw himself as a new Queen Elizabeth—or rather, being a humble man, as a regent for a new Queen Elizabeth; and he prepared, like her, to summon a series of deferential parliaments. Surely, since he was one of them, and since they all earnestly pursued the same honest ideal, the members would agree with him, just as they had agreed with 'that Lady, that great Queen'? Surely he had only to address them in the Painted Chamber, to commend them in a few eloquent phrases, to leave them to their harmonious deliberations, and then, having recieved from them a few 'good laws', to dismiss them, in due time, amid applause, complimentingly, with a 'Golden Speech'?

Alas, as we know, it did not happen thus. It was not with golden speeches that Cromwell found himself dismissing his parliaments, but with appeals to Heaven, torrents of abuse,—and force. This was not merely because the basis of legitimacy and consent were lacking: Queen Elizabeth, like Cromwell, was disputed in her title, and Cromwell, like Queen Elizabeth, was personally indispensable even to those extremists who chafed at his conservatism. The fatal flaw was elsewhere. Under Oliver Cromwell something was missing in the mechanics of parliamentary government. It was not merely that useful drop of oil with which Queen Elizabeth had now and then so gracefully lubricated the machine. It was something far more essential. To see what that omission was, we must turn from the character to the composition and working of those uniformly unfortunate assemblies.

The methods by which Queen Elizabeth so effectively controlled her parliaments of—for the most part—unpolitical gentry are now, thanks to the great work of Sir John Neale and Professor Notestein, well known.[1] They consisted, first, in electoral and other patronage and, secondly, in certain procedural devices among which the essential were two: the presence in parliament of a firm nucleus of experienced privy councillors, and royal control over the Speaker. Now these methods of control are of the greatest importance in the history of parlia-

[1] Wallace Notestein, *The Winning of the Initiative by the House of Commons* (British Academy Lecture, 1924); J. E. Neale, *The Elizabethan House of Commons* (1949); *Elizabeth I and her Parliaments.* (1953).

ment, and if we are to consider Oliver Cromwell as a parliamentarian it is necessary to consider his use both of this patronage and of these procedural devices. This, I think, has not before been attempted. My purpose in this essay is to attempt it. I believe it can be shown that it was precisely in this field that Cromwell's catastrophic failure as a parliamentarian lay. In order to show this it will be necessary to take Cromwell's parliaments in turn and to see, in each case, how far the patronage of the government and its supporters was used, and who formed that essential nucleus of effective parliamentary managers, that compact 'front-bench' which, under the Tudors, had been occupied by the royal privy council.

Of course, Cromwell did not inherit the system direct from Queen Elizabeth. In the intervening half-century there had been many changes—changes which had begun even before her death. For in the last years of Elizabeth both methods of royal control had been challenged: the puritans had developed a formidable parliamentary 'machine' independent of the privy council, and the Earl of Essex had sought to use aristocratic patronage to pack the House of Commons against the queen's ministers. But in the event, thanks to the parliamentary ability of the two Cecils, neither of these challenges had been successful. It was only after the death of the queen, and particularly after the rejection of Robert Cecil by James I, that the indifference of the Stuart kings and the incompetence of their ministers had enabled a parliamentary Opposition to develop and to organize both patronage and procedure against the Crown. By 1640, when the Long Parliament met, the tables had been completely turned. In that year the Opposition magnates—the Earls of Bedford,

Warwick and Pembroke—showed themselves better boroughmongers than the royal ministers, and the failure of Charles I to secure the election to parliament, for any constituency, of his intended Speaker could be described by Clarendon as 'an untoward and indeed an unheard of accident, which brake many of the king's measures and infinitely disordered his service beyond a capacity of reparation'. Thus in 1640 both patronage and procedure were firmly in the hands of the Opposition. But this turning of the tables did not entail any change in the system by which Parliament was operated. It merely meant that the same system which had formerly been operated by the Crown was now operated against it. John Pym, the ablest parliamentary manager since the Cecils, resumed their work. He controlled the patronage, the Speaker, and the front bench. From 1640 until 1643 parliament, in his hands, was once again an effective and disciplined body such as it had never been since 1603.

With the death of Pym in 1643, his indisputable empire over parliament dissolved and lesser men competed for its fragments. Vane and St. John among the radicals, Holles among the conservatives, emerged as party loaders; but they cannot be described as successful party leaders: the machine creaked and groaned, and it was only by disastrously calling in external force—the army—that Vane and St. John were able, in the end, to secure their control. On the other hand, once parliament had been purged and the king executed, a certain unity of counsel and policy returned. The Rump Parliament, which governed England from 1649 to 1653, may have been justly hated as a corrupt oligarchy, but it governed effectively, preserved the revolution, made and financed victorious war, and carried out a consistent policy of aggressive mercantile imperialism. Its rule was indeed the most systematic government of the Interregnum; and since this rule was the rule not of one known minister but of a number of overlapping assemblies operating now as parliament, now as committees of parliament, now as council of state, while some of the administrative departments were notoriously confused and confusing, it is reasonable to ask who were the effective managers who made this complex and anonymous junta work so forcefully and so smoothly. This is a question which, in my opinion, can be answered with some confidence.

We have, unfortunately, no private diaries of the Rump Parliament which can show who managed its business or debates, but we have later diaries which show at least who claimed to have managed them, and from this and other evidence I believe we can say that, at least after 1651, the policy of the Rump was controlled by a small group of determined and single-minded men. Up to the summer of 1651 the ascendancy of these men is not so apparent, but with the policy which prevailed after that date it can, I think, be clearly seen. For in 1651, with the passing of the Navigation Act and the declaration of war against the Netherlands, the old Elizabethan ideal of a protectorate over the Netherlands was jettisoned in favour of a new and opposite policy, a policy of mercantile aggression against a neighbouring Protestant power. Furthermore, this policy, we are repeatedly told, was the policy not of the whole parliament but of 'a very small number', with allies in the City of London, 'some few men' acting 'for their own interest', 'some few persons deeply interested in the East India trade and the new Plantations.'

Now the identity of these few men, or at least of their parliamentary managers, can hardly be doubted, for they never tired of naming themselves. They were Sir Arthur Hesilrige and Thomas Scot. In the later parliaments of the Interregnum, whose proceedings are fortunately known to us, Hesilrige and Scot appear as an inseparable and effective parliamentary combine. . . . Hesilrige and Scot were not only republicans. They were also, to use a later term, 'whigs'. If republics were to them the best of all forms of government, that was not merely because of classical or biblical precedents, nor because of the iniquity of particular kings: it was because republics alone, in their eyes, were the political systems capable of commercial empire. Like the later whigs, who were also accused of a preference for 'oligarchy', they found their great example in the mercantile republic of. Venice. . . .

Now it is interesting to note that this policy, the 'whig' policy of mercantile aggression which I have ascribed to Hesilrige and Scot and their allies in the City, though it was carried out by an 'Independent' parliament carefully purged of unsympathetic elements, was flatly contradictory to the declared views and prejudices of those ordinary Independent gentry whom Cromwell represented and who, in their general attitude, foreshadowed rather the tory squires than the mercantile whig pressure-group of the next generation. . . .

Thus the policy of the Rump in the years 1651–3—the years, that is, when the army's resentment was mounting against it—was not only the policy of a small managing group which had obtained control of the assembly: it was also a policy essentially opposed to the aims of those Independents who had made the revolution. For all their insistence upon decentralization, social justice and Protestant alliances, those Independents had proved quite incapable of making such a policy even in their own parliament which their own leader had purged in their interest. Unable, or unfitted, to exercise political power, they seemed doomed to surrender it to any organized group, however small, which was capable of wielding it—even if that group only used it to pursue policies quite different from their own. Though the 'tory' Independents had made the revolution and, through the army, held power in the state, the 'whigs' had contrived to secure power in parliament. To correct this and create a government of their own, the Independents had the choice between two policies. Either they could preserve the republican constitution and beat the 'whigs' at their own game—or, if that was too difficult for natural back-benchers, they could remove their rivals by force and place over parliament a 'single person', like-minded with themselves, to summon, dismiss and, above all, guide and regulate their assemblies. This latter course was entirely consistent with their general political philosophy; it was also the easier course; and consequently they took it. The crucial question was, did the new 'single person' understand the technique of his task? He had in his hands all the power of the state; but had he in his head the necessary knowledge of parliamentary management? That is, patronage and procedure to prevent another usurpation of the vacant front benches? Would he now fill them with his privy councillors and thus cement, as Queen Elizabeth had done, the natural harmony between the faithful, if somewhat inarticulate, Commons and the Throne? . . .

The evidence for this is sadly plain. For what was in the minds of Cromwell and his conservative allies when they decided, or agreed, to summon the Barebones Parliament? We look, and all we find is a well-meaning, devout, bewildered obscurity. The Independents had no political theories: believing that forms of government were indifferent, they counted simply on working with the existing institutions, and now that the existing institutions—first monarchy, then republic—had been destroyed, they were at a loss. 'It was necessary to pull down this government,' one of them had declared on the eve of the expulsion, 'and it would be time enough then to consider what should be placed in the rooms of it'; and afterwards it was officially stated that 'until the Parliament was actually dissolved, no resolutions were taken in what model to case the government, but it was after that dissolution debated and discussed as 'res integra'. In other words, having expelled the Rump Parliament which had betrayed the Independent cause, the Independent officers found themselves in a quandary. They had acted, as Cromwell so often acted, not rationally nor with that machiavellian duplicity with which his victims generally credited him, but on an impulse; and when the impulsive gesture had been made and the next and more deliberate step must be taken, they were quite unprepared.

Over the unprepared the prepared always have an advantage. In this case the prepared were the new radical party which had replaced the broken Levellers: the extreme totalitarian radicals, the Anabaptists and their fighting zealots the Fifth Monarchy Men. These men had already established themselves in the army through their disciplined tribunes, the chaplains; they already control many of the London pulpits; and for the capture of direct power they had two further assets: an organization, in the form of the Committee for the Propagation of the Gospel in Wales, which was now totally controlled by their energetic Welsh leader, Vavasour Powell, and his itinerant missionaries; and a patron at the highest level in Major-General Harrison, the commissioner in charge of the Welsh Propagators and—what was now more important—the alter ego of the unsuspecting Cromwell. . . .

As so often in the history of Oliver Cromwell, there is something at once tragic and comic in the manner of his deception by the Fifth Monarchy Men. To him they were merely good religious men, and when he found that his own exalted mood of indignation against the Rump was shared by them, he followed their advice, little suspecting what deeplaid political schemes lurked behind their mystical language. 'Reformation of law and clergy': was not that precisely his programme? A milder, cheaper, quicker law, a decentralized, godly, puritan clergy; were not these his ambitions? How was he to know that by the same phrase the 'Anabaptists' meant something quite different and far more radical: wholesale changes in the law of property, abolition of tithe, the extension over England of the closely organized, indoctrinated religious tribunes who had already carried their gospel over Wales 'like fire in the thatch'? Oliver Cromwell suspected no such thing. When Harrison urged him to expell the Rump as the persecutors of the 'poor saints in Wales', he innocently acquiesced; and when the refusal of the Rump to renew their authority had still left the Welsh Propagators without a legal basis, he as innocently supplied them with a substitute, writing to them to ignore strict legality and 'to go on cheerfully in the work as formerly, to promote these good things.' Months afterwards the greatest crime of the Rump would still seem to him to be its attempt to disband those Welsh Propagators, 'the poor people of God there, who had men watching over them like so many wolves, ready to catch the lamb as soon as it was brought out into the world'. This romantic view of a knot of Tammany demagogues, who concealed their sharp practices behind lachrymose Celtic oratory, was soon to be sadly dispelled.

As soon as they had secured the expulsion of the Rump, the Fifth Monarchy Men were ready for the next step. What they required was a legislature nominated by the supposedly 'independent' churches, some of which had been completely penetrated and were now safely controlled by them. Only in this way could so unrepresentative a party achieve power. Therefore when Cromwell remained poised in doubt, he soon found himself besieged by willing and unanimous advisers. . . .

Thus the Barebones Parliament was 'elected', and when it met, on 4 July 1653, Cromwell addressed it in his most exalted style. Now at last, he thought, he had a parliament after his heart, a parliament of godly men, gentry of his own kind, back-benchers, not scheming politicians—with a sprinkling, of course, of Saints . . . The results were as might have been expected. The Cromwellian back-benchers were as clumsy old bluebottles caught in the delicate web spun by nimble radical spiders. The radicals were few—there were only eighteen definitely identifiable Baptists or Fifth Monarchy Men, of whom five were from Wales; but it was enough. They made a dash for the crucial committees; Harrison, unlike Cromwell, sat regularly both in the House and on its committees; and outside the clerical organizers of the party had the London pulpits tuned. . . . Within six months the radicals had such control over the whole assembly that the Cromwellian conservatives, panic-stricken at their revolutionary designs, came early and furtively to Whitehall and surrendered back to the Lord General the powers which through lack of direction, they had proved incapable of wielding.

Who were the parliamentary managers of the Barebones Parliament who thus filled the vacuum left by Cromwell's inability or refusal to form a party? Once again, I think, they can be identified. Arthur Squibb, a Fifth Monarchy Man, was a London lawyer with Welsh connexions, and Samuel Moyer, a Baptist, was a London Financier and member of the East India Company who had recently been added—no doubt by Harrison—to the council of state. . . .

It was by force, in the end, that the little group of radicals who refused to accept the suicide of the majority were expelled. . . .

Cromwell's reply to the collapse of the Barebones Parliament was not to devise—he never devised anything—but to accept a new constitution. Just as, after his impulsive dismissal of the Rump, he had accepted the ready-made plans of Major-General Harrison and his party of Saints for a parliament of their nominees, so now, after the sudden disintegration of that parliament, he accepted from Major-General Lambert and his party of conservative senior officers the newly prefabricated constitution of the Instrument of Government. By this the new Protectorate was set up, and Cromwell, as Lord Protector, carefully limited by a council of senior officers, was required, after an interval of nine months, to summon a new parliament based on a new franchise. This new franchise was, basically, the realization of the plan already advanced by the conservative senior officers seven years earlier in Ireton's *Heads of Proposals,* it must be briefly analysed: for if

ever the Independent gentry got the kind of parliament for which they had fought, it should have been in the two parliaments of the Protectorate elected on the franchise which they had thus consistently advocated. If social composition were sufficient to secure a harmonious and working parliament, that success should now be assured. . . .

Cromwell's parliaments under the new franchise contained no English peers and very few merchants. They were parliaments of gentry, and not necessarily of the richer gentry either. The chief difference between the new and the old members was that whereas the old had been predominantly borough gentry the new were predominantly county gentry. What does this difference between 'borough gentry' and 'county gentry', in fact, mean?

A glance at English parliamentary history at any time between 1559 and 1832 provides the answer. The borough gentry were client gentry; the county gentry were not—they were, or could be independent of patronage. It was largely through the boroughs that patrons and parliamentary managers had, in the past, built up their forces in parliament. It was through them that Essex had built up a party against Cecil and Cecil against Essex, through them that Charles I might have resisted the Opposition magnates and the Opposition magnates were, in fact, able to resist him. Further, at all times, it was through the boroughs that able men—lawyers, officials, scholars—got into parliament as the clients of greater men and provided both the Administration and the Opposition with some of their most effective members. The 'rotten' boroughs, in fact, performed two functions: first, they made parliament less representative of the electors than it would otherwise have been; secondly, they made it less inefficient as an instrument of policy.

Now, if, as I have suggested, the 'Independent' gentry were, in fact, the rural 'back-bench' gentry, such as were afterwards represented in the tory party of Queen Anne and the first two Georges, it is clear that they, like the later tories, would be opposed to the borough system as being, by definition, a device of the front-bench politicians to evade the 'equal representation' of 'the people'—that is, of the country gentry—and to introduce 'courtiers' instead of honest country gentry into parliament. . . . Their philosophy was genuinely held: experience had not yet shown the inherent impossibility of a completely back-bench parliament or the inherent difficulty of decentralization by a revolutionary central government; and Cromwell no doubt supposed that honest, Independent country gentlemen, freely elected from within the puritan fold, would naturally agree with the aims and methods of his rule. . . .

A parliament of congenial, unorganized, Independent county gentry, likeminded with himself, reinforced by sixty direct nominees and saved, by the franchise, from the knavish tricks of rival electioneers—surely this would give Cromwell the kind of parliament he wanted. . . .

Able men can work any system, and even under the new franchise the experienced republicans had contrived to re-enter parliament. Once in, they moved with effortless rapidity into the vacuum created by the Protector's virtuous but misguided refusal to form a party. The speed with which they operate is astonishing: one is forced to conclude either that Hesilrige and Scot were really brilliant tacticians (a conclusion which the re-

corded evidence hardly warrants), or that Cromwell had no vestige of an organization to resist them. At the very beginning they nearly got their nominee —the notorious regicide Richard Bradshaw—in as Speaker. Having failed, they displaced the rival Speaker by the old dodge of calling for a Committee of the Whole House. At once Hesilrige and Scot were in control of the debates; the floating voters drifted helplessly into their wake; and the whole institution of the Protectorate came under heavy fire. Within a week Cromwell had repented of his words about 'a free Parliament', and all the republican members, with Hesilrige, Scot and Bradshaw at their head, had been turned out by force. Legislation was then handed back to the real back-benchers for whom the parliament had been intended.

Ironically, the result was no better. Again and again Cromwell, by his own refusal to organize and his purges of those who organized against him, created in parliament a vacuum of leadership; again and again this vacuum was filled. A pure parliament of back-benchers is an impossibility: someone will always come to the front; and since Cromwell never, like the Tudors, placed able ministers on the front benches, those benches were invariably occupied from behind. The first to scramble to the front were always the republicans: they were the real parliamentary tacticians of the Interregnum. But when they were removed, a second group advanced into their place. It was this second group who now, by their opposition, wrecked Cromwell's first Protectorate parliament.

Who were they? As we look at their programme, shown in their long series of successive amendments to the new constitution which had been imposed upon them, we see that, basically, it is the programme of the old 'country party' of 1640. The voice that emerges from those 'pedantic' amendments, as Carlyle so contemptuously called them, is the voice of the original opponents of Charles I, the voice even of Cromwell himself in his days of opposition. It protests, not, of course, against the decentralization which by his ordinances he had been carrying out, which was still his policy, and of which the new franchise itself was one expression, but against the machinery of centralization whereby this policy was declared: against the new court, the new arbitrariness, the new standing army, the new taxes of that Man of Blood, Oliver Cromwell. Cromwell was caught up in the necessities and contradictions of power and found himself faced by his own old colleagues in opposition. In his days of opposition he too, like them, had demanded a parliament of back-benchers. Now he had got it—when he was in power. By a new franchise and a new purge he had confined parliament to the old 'country party' just at the time when he had himself inherited the position, the difficulties and the necessities of the old court.

But who were the leaders who gave expression and direction to this new country party? A study of the tellers in divisions, which is almost all the evidence we possess, enables us to name the most active of them. There was John Bulkley, member for Hampshire, Sir Richard Onslow, member for Surrey, and, above all, Colonel Birch, member for Hereford; and the interesting fact about these men is that they were all old 'presbyterians". . . .

A fortnight later the Protector, now dependent entirely on the army officers, came suddenly down to Westminster prematurely to dissolve yet another parliament. 'I do not know what you have

been doing' he declared, 'I do not know whether you have been alive or dead'!—it is difficult to conceive of Queen Elizabeth or Lord Burghley making such an admission—and with the usual flood of turbid eloquence, hysterical abuse and appeals to God, he dissolved prematurely, what was to have been his ideal parliament.

For the next year Cromwell surrendered entirely to his military advisers. He still hankered after his old ideals—it is a great mistake, I think, to suppose that he ever 'betrayed' the revolution, or at least the revolution for which he had taken up the sword. But he resigned himself to the view that those ideals could best be secured by administration, not legislation. After all, 'forms of government' were to him indifferent: one system was as good as another, provided it secured good results; and now it seemed to him that the ideals of the revolution honest rule such as 'suits a Commonwealth', social justice, reform of the law, toleration—would be better secured through the summary but patriarchal rule of the major-generals than through the legal but wayward deliberations of even an Independent parliament.

The major-generals, like the Laudian bishops, might seek to supervise J. P.'s, to reform manners, to manage preachers, to resist enclosures; but all this was expensive, and when the Spanish war, like Laud's Scottish war, proved a failure, the major-generals themselves begged Cromwell, for financial reasons, to do what even Laud had had to do: to face a parliament. . . . Confident, as military men so often are, of their own efficiency, they assured him that they, unlike the bishops, could control the elections and secure a parliament which would give no trouble. So, in the autumn of 1656, after the most vigorous electioneering campaign since 1640, a parliament was duly elected.

The result was not at all what the major-generals had expected. Ironically, one of the reasons for their failure was that very reduction of the borough seats which the Independents had themselves designed. In the interest of decentralization, Cromwell and his friends had cut down a system of patronage which now at last they had learnt how to use. . . .

Thus, in spite of vigorous efforts to pack it, Cromwell's second and last Protectorate parliament consisted largely of the same persons as its predecessor; and in many respects its history was similar. Once again the old republicans had been returned: once again, as not being 'persons of known integrity, fearing God and of good conversation', they were arbitrarily removed. Once again the old backbenchers, the civilians, the new country party, filled the vacuum. But there was one very significant difference. It was a difference of leadership and policy. For this time they were not led by the old presbyterians. A new leadership appeared with a new policy, and the Independents now found themselves mobilized not against but for the government of Oliver Cromwell. Instead of attacking him as a 'single person', they offered now to support him as king.

The volte-face seems complete, and naturally many were surprised by it; but, in fact, it is not altogether surprising. The new policy was simply the old policy of Sir Anthony Ashley Cooper, the policy of civilizing Cromwell's rule by reverting to known institutions and restoring, under a new dynasty, not, of course, the government of the Stuarts, but the old system from which the Stuarts had so disastrously deviated. For after all, the Independents had not originally revolted against monarchy: the 'whig' republicans, who now claimed to be the heirs of the revolution, had, in fact, been belated up-

starts in its course, temporary usurpers of its aims. The genuine 'tory' Independents, who had now re-asserted themselves over those usurpers, had merely wanted a less irresponsible king than Charles I. Nor had they wanted new constitutions. They had no new doctrines; they merely wanted an old-style monarch like Queen Elizabeth. Why should they not now, after so many bungled alternatives, return to those original limited aims? Why should not Cromwell, since he already exercised monarchical power, adjust himself more completely to a monarchical position? In many ways the policy of the 'Kingship party' in parliament—however denounced by the republicans as a betrayal of the revolution which they sought to corner—was, in fact, the nearest that the puritans ever got to realizing their original aims. Consequently it found wide support. The 'country party' and the new court at last came together.

Who was the architect of this parliamentary coup? There can be no doubt about his identity. Once again, it was a former royalist. Lord Broghill, a son of the first Earl of Cork, was an Irish magnate who had become a personal friend and supporter of Cromwell. He was now member of parliament for County Cork, and his immediate supporters were the other members for Ireland, whom, no doubt, as Cromwell's Irish confidant, he had himself helped to nominate. . . .

Once again the remarkable thing is the case with which the new leadership secured control over parliament. Just as the eleven 'presbyterian' leaders, whenever they were allowed to be present in 1647–8, had always been able to win control of the Long Parliament from Vane and St. John; just as, after 1649, the little group of republicans dominated every parliament to which they were admitted; just as a score of radical extremists dominated the Barebones Parliament of 1653, or a handful of old presbyterians the Purged Parliament of 1654, so the little group of 'Kingship-men' quickly took control, against the protesting major-generals, of the parliament of 1656. Their success illustrated the complete absence of any rival organization, any organization by the Government—and, incidentally, the ease with which Cromwell, if he had taken the trouble or understood the means, could have controlled such docile parliaments. . . .

Having captured a majority in parliament, the Kingship party set methodically to work. The government of the major-generals was abolished; the kingship, and the whole political apparatus which went with it—House of Lords, privy council, State Church, and old parliamentary franchise—was proposed. Except for the army leaders, whom such a policy would have civilized out of existence, and the obstinate, doctrinaire republicans, all political groups were mobilized. The officials, the lawyers, the Protectoral family and clients, the government financiers—all who had an interest in the stability of government—were in favour. At last, it seemed, Cromwell had an organized party in parliament. He had not made it: it had made itself and presented itself to him ready-made. It only asked to be used. What use did Cromwell make of it?

The answer is clear. He ruined it. Unable to win over the army leaders, he wrestled with them, rated them, blustered at them. 'It was time', he protested, 'to come to a settlement and leave aside these arbitrary measures so unacceptable to the nation.' and then, when he found them inexorable, he surrendered to them and afterwards justified his surrender in parliament by describing not the interested opposition of serried brass-hats but the alleged honest scruples of religious nonconformist sergeants. Of course, he may have been right to yield. Perhaps he judged the balance of power correctly. Perhaps he could not have maintained his new monarchy without army support. There was here a real dilemma. And yet the army could certainly have been 're-modelled'—purged of its politicians and yet kept strong enough to defend the new dynasty . . . Cromwell's own personal ascendancy over the army, apart from a few politically ambitious generals, was undisputed. Instead of pleading defensively with the 'army grandees' as an organized party, he could have cashiered a few of them silently, as examples to the rest, and all opposition to kingship would probably have evaporated; for it was nourished by his indecision. The total eclipse first of Harrison, then of Lambert, once they had been dismissed—though each in turn had been second man in the army and the State—sufficiently shows the truth. . . .

Be that as it may, Cromwell never, in fact, tried to solve the problem of army opposition. After infinite delays and a series of long speeches, each obscurer than the last, he finally surrendered to it and accepted the new constitution only in a hopelessly truncated form: without kingship, without Lords, without effective privy council. Even so, in the view of Lord Broghill and his party, it might have been made to work. But again, Cromwell would not face the facts. Neither in his new Upper House nor in his new council would he give the Kingship-men the possibility of making a party. Spasmodic, erratic gestures now raised, now dashed their hopes, and led ultimately nowhere; the leaders of the party wrung their hands in despair at the perpetual indecision, the self-contradictory gestures of their intended king; and in the end, in January

1658, when the parliament reassembled for its second session, the old republicans, re-admitted under the new constitution, and compacted by their long exile, found the Kingship-men a divided, helpless, dispirited group, utterly at their mercy.

At once they seized their opportunity. The lead was given by their old leader, Sir Arthur Hesilrige. . . . Within ten days all constructive business had become impossible: the parliament, the French ambassador reported to his Government, 'était devenu le parlemant de Hesilrige', and as such Cromwell angrily dissolved it, 'and God judge between you and me'. Before he could summon another, he was dead.

Oliver Cromwell's parliaments were thus consistently hamstrung through lack of direction. . . . Successive efforts to govern with an through parliament failed, and failed abjectly. They failed through lack of that parliamentary management by the executive which, in the correct dosage, is the essential nourishment of any sound parliamentary life. As always with Cromwell, there is an element of tragic irony in his failure: his very virtues caused him to blunder into courses from which he could escape only by the most unvirtuous, inconsistent and indefensible expendients. And the ultimate reason of this tragic, ironical failure lies, I think, in the very character of Cromwell and of the Independency which he so perfectly represented. Cromwell himself, like his followers, was a natural back-bencher. He never understood the subtleties of politics, never rose above the simple political prejudices of those other backwoods squires whom he had joined in their blind revolt against the Stuart court. His first speech in parliament had been the protest of a provincial squire against popish antics in his own parish church; and at the end, as ruler of three kingdoms,

he still compared himself only with a bewildered parish-constable seeking laboriously and earnestly to keep the peace in a somewhat disorderly and incomprehensible parish. His conception of government was the rough justice of a benevolent, serious-minded, rural magistrate: well-intentioned, unsophisticated, summary, patriarchal conservative. Such was also the political philosophy of many other English squires, who, in the seventeenth century, turned up in parliament and, sitting patiently on the back benches, either never understood or, at most, deeply suspected the secret mechanism whereby the back benches were controlled from the front. In ordinary times the natural fate of such men was to stay at the back, and to make a virtue of their 'honesty', their 'independency', their kinship rather with the good people who had elected them than with the sharp politicians and courtiers among whom they found themselves. But the 1640's and 1650's were not ordinary times. Then a revolutionary situation thrust those men forward, and in their indignation they hacked down, from behind, the sharp politicians and courtiers, the royalists and presbyterians, who had first mobilized them. Having no clear political ideas, they did not—except in the brief period when they surrendered to the republican usurpers—destroy institutions, but only persons. They destroyed parliamentarians and the king, but not parliament or the throne. These institutions, in their fury, they simply cleaned out and left momentarily vacant. . . .

Alas, in political matters natural harmony is not enough. To complete the system, and to make it work, something else was necessary too: an Independent political caucus that would constitute an Independent front bench as a bridge between crown and parliament, like those

Tudor privy councillors who gave consistency and direction to the parliaments of Henry VIII and Elizabeth. Unfortunately this was the one thing which Cromwell always refused to provide. To good Independents any political caucus was suspect: it smacked of sharp politicians and the court. An Independent front bench was a contradiction in terms. Even those who, in turn, and without his support, sought to create such a front bench for him—Sir Anthony Ashley Cooper, Sir Charles Wolseley, Lord Broghill—were not real Independents but, all of them, ex-royalists. Like his fellow-squires (and like those liberal historians who virtuously blame the Tudors for 'packing' their parliaments), Cromwell tended to regard all parliamentary management as a 'cabal', a wicked interference with the freedom of parliament. Therefore he supplied none, and when other more politically-minded men sought to fill the void, he intervened to crush such indecent organization. In this way he thought he was securing 'free parliaments' —free, that is, from caucus-control. Having thus secured a 'free parliament', he expected it automatically, as a result merely of good advice, good intentions and goodwill, to produce 'good laws', as in the reign of his heroine Queen Elizabeth. He did not realize that Queen Elizabeth's parliaments owed their effectiveness not to such 'freedom', nor to the personal worthiness of the parties, nor the natural harmony between them, but to that ceaseless vigilance, intervention and management by the privy council which worthy puritan back-benchers regarded as a monstrous limitation of their freedom. No wonder Cromwell's parliaments were uniformly barren. His ideal was an Elizabethan parliament, but his methods were such as would lead to a Polish Diet.

Consequently, each of his parliaments, deprived of leadership from him, fell in turn under other leadership and were then treated by him in a manner which made them feel far from free. Only in Cromwell's last year did a Cromwellian party-manager, without encouragement from him, emerge in the House of Commons and seek to save the real aims of the revolution; but even he, having been tardily accepted, was ultimately betrayed by his inconstant master. In that betrayal Cromwell lost what proved to be his last chance of achieving the 'settlement' which he so long and so faithfully but so unskilfully pursued.

Thus it is really misleading to speak of 'Cromwell and his parliaments' as we speak of 'Queen Elizabeth and her parliaments', for in that possessive sense Cromwell—to his misfortune—had no parliaments: he only faced, in a helpless, bewildered manner, a succession of parliaments which he failed either to pack, to control or to understand. There was the parliament of Hesilrige and Scot, the parliament of Squibb and Moyer, the parliament of Birch, the parliament of Broghill, and the parliament of Hesilrige once again; but there was never a parliament of Oliver Cromwell. Ironically, the one English sovereign who had actually been a member of parliament proved himself, as a parliamentarian, the most incompetent of them all. He did so because he had not studied the necessary rules of the game. Hoping to imitate Queen Elizabeth, who, by understanding those rules, had been able to play upon 'her faithful Commons' like a well-tuned instrument, he failed even more dismally than the Stuarts. The tragedy is that whereas they did not believe in the system, he did.

CHRISTOPHER HILL (1912–   ) is Master of
Balliol College, Oxford, and the leading living scholar
of the Stuart period. Earlier a left-winger and economic
determinist, his mature work is both intricate and
subtle, marked by voracious reading and delicate
analysis. Hill explores most brilliantly the
interrelationships between social needs, political events,
religion, and culture. He has a sharp yet sympathetic
eye for the ambivalence of human motivation and for
the mundane interest served by ethereal theorizing.
In this extract, he relates what seems paradoxical in
Cromwell's behavior to the complex needs of his
political and social situation. Mr. Hill's latest
biography of Cromwell, called *God's Englishman*
(London, 1970), adds flesh and fuller detail to the
skeletonic sketch below.*

Christopher Hill

Paradoxes of Personality and Revolution

Ever since the death of Oliver Cromwell 300 years ago his reputation has been the subject of controversy . . . There can be such varying interpretations of Oliver's character, motives and place in history because his character and actions bristle with paradoxes. . . .

(1) First is the paradox . . . that the revolutionary of the 'forties became the conservative dictator of the 'fifties. At a time when Parliament claimed to be fighting *for* the King *against* his evil counsellors, Cromwell was reported as saying that "if the King were before me I would shoot him as another;" and that he hoped to live to see never a nobleman in England. He was "the darling of the sectaries," and he played the lead-

ing part in bringing Charles I to the scaffold. Yet Cromwell was no theoretical republican. He was described as "king-ridden;" in 1652 he asked "What if a man should take upon him to be King?"; in 1657 monarchy was virtually restored, with the Lord Protector as monarch. By that date his former radical allies had broken with him — Lilburne in 1649, Harrison in 1653, Lambert in 1657. George Fox thought Oliver deserved the ignominious treatment he received at the Restoration because he failed to keep his promise to abolish tithes.

(2) Closely allied is Cromwell's attitude to constitutional government. He organized an army to fight for Parliament against the King. He sponsored the Self-

*From Christopher Hill, *Oliver Cromwell, 1658–1958,* Historical Association Pamphlet No. 38. Used by permission of the author and the Publications Committee of the Historical Association.

Denying Ordinance which ordered all members of the two houses to lay down their military commands: yet Oliver alone retained his. In 1647, though he tried to mediate between Parliament and Army, in the last resort he sided with the Army in every crisis. In December 1648 he acquiesced in the Army's purge of Parliament; in 1653 he himself used the Army to dissolve Parliament. Except as Lord General he would never have become Protector. Yet from 1654 onwards he aimed, apparently genuinely, at a "settlement" by which the military basis of his rule would be ended, and a parliamentary constitution established: and was defeated in this aim by his Army. "What's for their good, not what pleases them," had been his object in 1647. In the 'fifties he could claim to be imposing liberty by the means of tyranny. Through the Major-Generals he enforced a greater degree of religious toleration than any Parliament elected on a propertied franchise could approve of. "'Tis against the will of the nation," Calamy said of the Protectorate; "there will be nine in ten against you." "But what," Oliver replied, "if I should disarm the nine, and put a sword in the tenth man's hand? Would not that do the business?"

(3) Another paradox is to be found in his attitude towards those unrepresented in Parliament. Promotion in his Army went by merit, regardless of social or political considerations. "I had rather have a plain russet-coated captain that knows what he fights for, and loves what he knows, than that which you call a gentleman and is nothing else." "It had been well that men of honour and birth had entered into these employments, but why do they not appear? . . . But seeing it was necessary the work must go on, better plain men than none." "The state, in choosing men to serve them,

takes no notice of their opinions; if they be willing faithfully to serve them, that satisfies." Cromwell was appealing, consciously if reluctantly, to the lower classes for the fighting support his own class had failed to give. Yet he opposed the Leveller demand for manhood suffrage. In his speeches to his first Parliament he equated poor men with bad men, and said that if a Commonwealth must suffer, it was better that it should suffer from the rich than from the poor. The Levellers, with whom he worked in 1647 and in the winter of 1648–9, and whose leaders he imprisoned and shot in the spring of 1649, had some reason to regard Cromwell as a double-crosser.

(4) Even in those political convictions which he most strongly and genuinely held there are obvious contradictions. Cromwell wrote to the General Assembly of the Kirk of Scotland: "I beseech you in the bowels of Christ, think it possible you may be mistaken," and said to the Governor of Edinburgh Castle, in words that shocked many nineteenth-century nonconformists, "Your pretended fear lest error should step in, is like the man that would keep all the wine out of the country lest men should be drunk." Yet he justified the massacre of Irish Catholics at Drogheda as "a righteous judgment of God upon these barbarous wretches," and said: "if by liberty of conscience you mean a liberty to exercise the mass . . . where the Parliament of England have power, that will not be allowed."

(5) Cromwell was not a hypocrite. And yet he sometimes comes very near hypocrisy in the absoluteness of his self-deception. "He will weep, howl and repent, even while he doth smite you under the first rib," wrote men who had some experience of Oliver's methods.

The Irish have always found it difficult to take at its face value his declaration that "We come (by the assistance of God) to hold forth and maintain the lustre and glory of English liberty in a nation where we have an undoubted right to it; wherein the people of Ireland . . . may equally participate in all benefits, to use liberty and fortune equally with Englishmen, if they keep out of arms." Cromwell was never quite sure whether his main duty was to the people of England or to the people of God. He assumed that "the interest of Christians" was identical with "the interest of the nation," but not all the "ungodly" majority would have agreed. Thurloe, Oliver's secretary, on one occasion differentiated sharply between the "vile levelling party" and "the good and goley." In Cromwell's foreign policy Firth saw a mixture of commercial traveller and Puritan Don Quixote. Cromwell always talked of the Protestant interest; but it is difficult to think of a single instance in which he supported protestantism to the detriment of England's political and commercial interests. His famous intervention on behalf of the Vaudois seems to have done the persecuted heretics little good in the long run; but it was excellent for England's prestige, and helped to force France to conclude the treaty of October 1655. In the Baltic Oliver advocated a Protestant alliance; but it was when Charles X threatened to establish Swedish power on both sides of the Sound, to the detriment of English trade, that the Protector most persistently sought to divert his energies into attacking papist Austrians and Poles. We all know of the famous scene at Whitelocke's departure for Sweden, when Oliver adjured him: "Bring us back a Protestant alliance!" But we shall search in vain in the official instructions given to Whitelocke for any such ideological purpose. It is all sordid, commercial and diplomatic.

(6) Finally, Oliver curiously combines hesitation, waiting on the Lord, with sudden violent action. At many of the crises of the period he was either missing, or played a highly ambiguous role. In the first four months of 1647, when the quarrel between Parliament and Army was coming to a head, he took no part in the negotiations. To this day historians do not know how far, if at all, Cromwell authorized Joyce's seizure of the King at Holmby House in June 1647. We know only that after the seizure had occurred he threw in his lot with the revolutionary Army. At the time of Pride's Purge he was far away, apparently prolonging quite unnecessarily his stay at the siege of Pontefract. When he returned he said "he had not been acquainted with the design, but since it was done he was glad of it." Again in the winter of 1652–3 there were long delays and hesitations, and much criticism from his fellow-officers, before Cromwell finally lost his temper and dissolved the Long Parliament. "It hath been the way God hath dealt with us all along," he commented; "to keep things from our eyes, that in what we have acted we have seen nothing before us — which is also a witness, in some measure, to our integrity." Cromwell's share in the dissolution of the Bare-bones Parliament is shrouded in mystery. He denied solemnly that he knew beforehand what was going to happen; but he accepted the *fait accompli*. In 1657 there were interminable delays before the final rejection of kingship; and then in 1658 the final explosion, brushing Fleetwood's protest aside with "You are a milksop; by the living God I will dissolve the House!" The conversations recorded by political opponents like George Fox, Edmund Ludlow and

John Rogers make attractive reading because of Oliver's obvious sincerity; but those to whom he listened so attentively were often disappointed by his failure to adopt the point of view they had put before him. There is something mysterious about the way in which Oliver took his political decisions, about his mental processes. Did he control events, or did they control him?

Some of these contradictions can be explained by the accidents of Cromwell's personal history. He was far more tolerant than most men of his time and class. . . . Only in his intolerance towards Irish papists did Cromwell fail to rise above the standards of his age. But others of the paradoxes stem from specific features of the English Revolution and from the Puritan ideas which guided its leaders. To them we now turn.

The Calvinist doctrine of the church contains a fundamental ambiguity. In one sense the church is all the people in a given community; in another sense it is the elect only. For the elect, Calvinism was a doctrine of spiritual equality: any good man was better than a peer or a king who was not in a state of grace. Puritan preachers sometimes presented this as though it was a doctrine of human equality: the qualifications were not always insisted on as carefully as they should have been. It was easy for many laymen to proceed direct from Calvinism to Lilburnian democracy. But for the true Calvinist some men were undoubtedly more equal than others: the elect had privileges, rights and duties, because they were elect, which raised them head and shoulders above the sinful mass of mankind. In opposition the emphasis was on spiritual equality, with appropriate vagueness about the precise individuals who were equal: in

power Presbyterians naturally wished to subordinate and discipline the sinful masses. Yet a linguistic ambiguity remained, just as it remained in the vocabulary of Locke, who talked of "the people" in a dual sense: sometimes he meant all the inhabitants, at other times he meant the propertied class, and assumed that "the people" had servants. Those who loosely used Calvinist or Lockean language were liable to deceive those whose interpretation was stricter. The latter, in Wildman's expressive phrase at Putney, were "cozened, as we are like to be."

Cromwell can be identified with no sect. But he was a Calvinist, and thought democracy manifestly absurd. For those with "the root of the matter" in them, yes: for them no privileges were too great, no barriers should prevent them serving the state. But "the root of the matter," "the godly"—they are woefully imprecise phrases. In the moment of battle those who fight bravely on your side clearly have this root. But in peace visible saints are difficult to identify. It is easy to slip into interpreting "the root of the matter" to mean "agreeing with me;" then "disagreeing with me" comes to mean "ensnared by fleshly reasonings". . . . This tendency within Puritanism towards an ultimate anarchy of individual consciences seemed to Cromwell to justify military dictatorship as the only means of preserving the essential gains of the Cause. He came to see himself as the unwilling constable set not only over the people of England, but even over the good people in England.

Calvinism was one formative influence. Cromwell's own political experience was another. At Huntingdon in the sixteen-thirties he opposed the transformation of the town council into a close oligarchy, and helped to protect the rights of poorer burgesses. An early letter shows him pleading with a London merchant for continuance of money to maintain a lectureship "in these times wherin we see they are suppressed with too much haste and violence by the enemies of God his truth." On behalf of fenmen whose common rights were endangered he opposed the drainage of the Fens by the Earl of Bedford and his associates. This was no mere philanthropic gesture. Cromwell arranged, in a business-like manner, contributions from all the commoners affected, with which he promised to hold the drainers in suit for five years. His attitude appears to have been inherited with his estates: his uncle had also opposed fen drainage. So we have here something more than an accident of personal biography — kindness of heart, or factious opposition. Common material interests linked a section of the gentry with humbler countrymen against privileged great landlords exploiting court influence. As "Lord of the Fens" Oliver was already occupying in his county a political position similar to that which he held nationally a decade later: the country gentlemen leading freeholders and people against courtiers and peers. In both cases his stand was liable to be misunderstood. Leader and led seemed to have identical aims when they only had common enemies. . . .

In 1640–2 diverse groups were united against the government. Commoners, yeomen and some gentlemen opposed enclosing landlords and court patentees. Congregations, led by their richer members, looked to London merchants to help them to get the preaching of which the hierarchy deprived them. Townsmen opposed royal attempts to remodel their government. Most men of property opposed arbitrary taxation; men and women of all classes opposed monopolies.

The House of Commons elected in the autumn of 1640 was not a revolutionary assembly. Elected on the traditional propertied franchise, the M.P.'s were a cross-section of the ruling class. Nevertheless, they had been elected under pressure of popular opposition occasioned by the final fiasco of the Scottish war. The wider the franchise in a constituency, the more likely were opponents of the court to be returned. But from 1641 the atmosphere began to change. In many counties there were enclosure riots, one of which Cromwell defended in the Commons; tenants began to refuse to pay rents; in London unruly crowds got into the habit of visiting Westminster to put pressure on M.P.s. Sectarian congregations emerged from their underground existence and began openly preaching seditious doctrines. In December 1641–January 1642, amid scenes suggestive of the French Revolution, the royalist clique of aldermen which controlled the City government was overthrown and replaced by radical Parliamentarians. Men of property began to have second thoughts. The King took heart, withdrew from London, and started to collect an army.

Gentlemen all over England tried hard to be neutral. But neutrality was increasingly difficult. As the King formed his army, all but the staunchest Parliamentarians in the North and West came to heel. Nearly 100 M.P.'s with estates in counties occupied by the royal forces changed to the King's side. They included a stalwart like John Dutton, M.P. for Gloucestershire, who had once endured imprisonment for the parliamentary cause; but not it was a matter of "the preservation of his house and estate." We can imagine how men of lesser conviction behaved. Many gentlemen, especially in the North and West, abandoned Parliament when opposition was pushed to the point of rebellion. These were the "constitutional royalists," of whom Hyde made himself the spokesman. A second consequence of the social anxiety of 1641–3 was the determination of most of the solid and respectable families supporting Parliament to end the war as quickly as possible. The initiative in *fighting* the King came from socially lower groups—from the clothing districts of the West Riding, which practically forced Fairfax to lead them into battle, and from towns like Manchester; from the "Moorlanders" in Staffordshire, who banded together with little help from the gentry, and were led by "a person of low quality." Within the familiar distinction between economically backward and royalist North and West, and economically advanced and parliamentarian South and East, we must also see a division between "compromise-peace" rich and "win-the-war" plebeians. The former are those whose representatives at Westminster we call "Presbyterians."

Their "Presbyterianism" had two essential features: (i) It was the price of the Scottish alliance; (ii) it envisaged the preservation of a national church, subordinated to the central control of Parliament and to the local control of the men of property (elders were nominated in the acts setting up presbyteries). As against the "presbyterian" desire for a limited war, fought by county militias officered by the local gentry (or by a professional Scottish army hired for the purpose), the "Independents" were prepared for a war without limits. "It must not be soldiers nor Scots that must

do this work," said Oliver Cromwell, "but it must be the godly." Religious toleration was the means of ensuring the widest possible unity among the Parliamentarians; for "religious toleration" in seventeenth-century terms meant freedom of assembly, discussion and organization.

So divisions at Westminster reflected divisions in the country. The counties which supported Parliament were run by committees composed of their leading gentry. As the war progressed, splits appeared in all those county committees which have so far been studied. The majority wished for a limited war, and concerned themselves mainly with safeguarding their own estates. A minority, drawn from those most active in the field, called for an all-out war. For organization and leadership they looked to London; for support they relied on lower social groups in their counties, outside the charmed circle of the ruling class. Sir William Brereton found that he had to replace the military governor of Stafford, who came from one of the best county families, by a rich Walsall merchant. Soon Brereton was heading a party in Staffordshire, composed of religious and political radicals, which aimed at taking control of the county away from the old families. In Kent and Nottinghamshire too, county government passed into the hands of social inferiors. . . .

Cromwell allowed his men complete freedom of political and religious discussion; appointments went by efficiency only, regardless of social rank. Contemporaries [even] alleged that Cromwell went out of his way to choose as officers "such as were common men, poor or of mean parentage." The logic of war brought Cromwell's principles, and Cromwell himself, to the top. . . . By the end of the war Cromwell had won a unique position. He was the idol of the Army, not only because he was a consistently successful general, but also because he had shown himself determined and courageous in sinking political differences for the sake of unity. . . .

The royalists had been beaten: the battle now began between the old ruling families, whose representatives sat in Parliament, and the civilians in uniform living on free quarter in the Home Counties. Cromwell, unique among Englishmen, had not only a foot in both camps, but a share in the strongest feelings of both sides. With the radicals and the Army he demanded toleration; with the conservatives he wanted to preserve existing social relations. "A nobleman, a gentleman, a yeoman: that is a good interest of the nation, and a great one". . . .

In May 1647 Cromwell and the officers threw in their lot with the rank and file. The result, Cromwell explained to the House of Commons, was to bring off "the soldiers from their late ways of correspondency and actings between themselves," and reduce them "towards a right order and regard to their officers." Six months of uneasy co-operation followed. . . . In debates in the Army Council at Putney which started at the end of October two conceptions of the future constitution of England confronted one another: the Heads of Proposals put forward by the Independent officers, and the Leveller Agreement of the People.

"Agreement of the People" is English for Social Contract. The Leveller theory was that in the civil war the old constitution had broken down; the Agreement was to refound the state on a new basis. Acceptance of the Agreement was to be necessary to citizenship, but all who accepted it should be free and equal citizens. The old property franchise

would be replaced by manhood suffrage. The Levellers had no intention of submitting the Agreement to Parliament; for Parliament was part of the defunct constitution whose breakdown had left England in the state of nature. So radical and revolutionary a solution appalled the generals, who came from the propertied class themselves. Many of them had received substantial grants of land from Parliament. Unlike the doctrinaire Ireton, Cromwell was prepared to consider concessions to Leveller views. Some copyholders by inheritance, perhaps, might be allowed the vote; though not wage labourers or recipients of alms. But to scrap the existing constitution, he thought, would be to throw too much into the melting-pot—law, order, property, social subordination and social stability.

The profound divergences revealed at Putney explain the policy adopted by Cromwell and the Independent Grandees towards the Levellers during the next two years. In November they broke decisively with them. . . . This break with the Levellers was a decisive moment in Oliver's career. Till then the Revolution had moved steadily to the left. Henceforth, unevenly at first, a reverse trend set in which ended only with the Restoration. . . .

[Returning] to the paradoxes of Oliver Cromwell, we may be able to see in them something more than the peculiarities of his personality. They were, I suggest, paradoxes of the English Revolution. All great revolutions are necessarily contradictory, ambiguous. They can begin only by a breach within the ruling class itself, a "revolt of the nobles." But in order to overthrow an old-established government and make profound changes in society, wider support is needed, especially from the unprivileged classes. To rouse them to effective political action, ideas have to be let loose which may prove inconvenient to those who later establish themselves in power. A halt at some stage has to be called: the more conservative revolutionaries break with their radical supporters, the Directory succeeds the Jacobins. The uniqueness of Cromwell is that he was Napoleon to his own Robespierre, Stalin to his own Lenin and Trotsky. Hence the accusations of self-seeking and treachery showered on him by the radicals who felt he had deceived them.

He had not deceived them. He may have deceived himself, but there was a dualism in his personality which made him the ideal leader of the revolt and the ideal leader of the Independents, those who first co-operated with the radicals and then led the move towards restabilization. Cromwell's passion for toleration aligned him with sectaries and Levellers against most of his own class; yet, despite his real interest in humanitarian law reform and his alleged hostility to tithes, he retained too many conservative prejudices to go far with the radicals. . . .

The paradox that Oliver's real tolerance did not extend to papists is no paradox at all if we recall that they had been "accounted, ever since I was born, Spaniolized". . . .

His foreign policy also loses some of its paradoxicality if regarded in historical perspective. The sixteen-fifties saw the beginning of that purposeful application of the resources of the state to commercial war and the struggle for colonies that characterized English foreign policy for the next 150 years. This was not Cromwell's personal policy. It goes back to Hakluyt, Ralegh, the Earl of Warwick—whose grandson married

the Lord Protector's daughter in 1657— and to the Providence Island Company which had supplied so many of the leaders of 1640. But it had never before been adopted as consistent government policy. . . . The paradox underlying Oliver's attitude to foreign affairs—the protestant interest or the interest of the nation—is not peculiar to him. . . . It had existed in the minds of Englishmen ever since Hakluyt advocated colonization of America for the good of the souls of Indians and the pockets of Englishmen. But God did seem to have put aces up the Protector's sleeve. . . . This is no place to discuss the psychological connections between Calvinism and the capitalist spirit. But the connections are deep and long-lived: they are paradoxes of the English Revolution itself.

Finally, the clue to Cromwell's delays and sudden violent actings is to be found in the famous maxim "Trust in God and keep your powder dry." Because one is fighting God's battles, one must be more, not less, careful to run no risk of failure. On the battlefield Cromwell rarely attacked until he had local military superiority. In politics, too, since the cause was the Lord's, every avenue must be explored, every contingency foreseen, before Cromwell committed himself to any course of action. In his periods of delay and hesitation Cromwell not only sought the Lord, he also consulted Ireton, Vane, Harrison, Lambert, Thurloe, Broghill—anyone whose opinion might be of significance. When he had completed his reconnaissance, and was sure of his dispositions, then he struck hard and with confidence that he was acting righteously. But to contemporaries "waiting on the Lord" might seem like waiting to see which way the cat would jump.

Again this is a paradox of Puritanism.

"Trust in God and keep your powder dry" perfectly expresses that tension between predestination and free will which lay at the heart of Calvinism. God has his purposes for this world which are pre-ordained; but God may act through human agents. . . . In the sixteen-forties not only Cromwell and Milton but thousands of lesser men had drawn tremendous moral energy from the conviction that God had chosen them to serve Him. Here again the explanation is ultimately social: problems exist, and certain men feel themselves qualified to solve them. It therefore becomes their duty to make their contribution to setting society right. A revolutionary situation breeds men with this sense of mission. Without them, revolutionary change could never take place; yet they would not act unless they were stimulated by the confidence that God, or Reason, or History, was on their side. . . . Here Oliver personifies not only the English Revolution but all great revolutions.

When the historian looks back at God's "working of things from one period to another" in the great turning-point of the seventeenth century, he will agree with Oliver that "such things . . . have not been known in the world these thousand years." But he has to add that it was the political, constitutional and economic revolutions that succeeded: the Puritan Revolution failed. And the Protectorate, . . . was the period in which this outcome became inevitable. Herein lies the final paradox, the historic irony and the personal tragedy of the career of Oliver Cromwell.

Educated in Australia, Canada, and England, JOHN
F. H. NEW (1936–   ) taught for some years in the
United States before returning to Canada where he is
now Professor and Chairman of a history department.
He is intrigued by the history and the influence of
religious ideas. In the article below, New traces the
sources of Cromwell's ambivalence to his Puritanism
rather than to social and political circumstances.*

John F. H. New

Cromwell and the Paradoxes of
Puritanism

[This note seeks] to prospect for sources
of ambivalence in Cromwell's theology,
to see whether they may throw light on
the ambiguities of his practise.

It could be objected that the better way
to understand Cromwell is "existentially
rather than essentially:" one should look
to his career rather than his creed and
analyse his specific decisions in the context of the crises that usually accompanied
them. But this approach has been tried
and tried again, and still the results are
inconclusive. It might be objected further
that to draw Puritanism in paradoxical
terms will not explain why Cromwell
chose one course rather than another in
any given situation. It is not intended that
it should for it is known that his class and
personal interests, his temperament and
prejudices, his colleagues, and associates
played upon him constantly. The influence of his theology is less specific,
and its cast not immediately apparent.
Some attempt, therefore, to reconstruct
his theology may contribute to an understanding of Oliver's mind.

Cromwell shared, first, the paradoxical
Puritan theology of the church.† On the
one hand, Puritans knew that the Church
was a human and a fallible institution,
and on the other they blurred the distinction between the visible and the invisible churches by assuming that the
Church on earth was composed of chosen

---

† The Puritan theology referred to here and throughout the essay is that of non-separating, orthodox, main-
line Puritanism. It is not intended to encompass the separatists' views: their theologies — the theologies of
Milton or Fox, for example — took rather different turns.

* From John F. H. New, "Oliver Cromwell and the Paradoxes of Puritanism," in *The Journal of British
Studies*, IV, No. 2 (May, 1965). Used by permission of the editor of *The Journal of British Studies*.

persons. In *The Way of the Churches of Christ in New England* John Cotton showed how liberal the New World churches were in receiving souls into their fellowship: "We do not exact eminent measure, either of knowledge or holiness, but do willingly stretch out our hands to recieve the weak in faith." Puritans knew very well that the visible church contained a good many backsliders, yet even though hypocrites might filter through the screening, the church as a whole was, and ought to be regarded as a gathering of visible saints. A century earlier Calvin had formulated precisely this attitude, stating that all members of the visible church "have become partakers with Christ, (and) are set apart as the proper and peculiar possession of God." A confusion of the visible and invisible bodies of Christ seems the most plausible explanation for the emphasis on the holy community in Puritanism. Church militant and Church triumphant did not merely overlap; Puritans thought of the two as being of one and the same glorious communion.

This collation of the human and the divine institutions necessarily enhanced the awareness of the community of saints. In Anglicanism that doctrine suggested a distant mystical link with the saints above, but in Puritanism it involved fellowship with the sanctified both past and present. It was the latter immanent sense that pervaded Puritanism. From it arose the urge to participate more fully as a fellowship in the motions of the church; and fragmentation followed in the wake of this increased congregationalism. Independency represents the rationalization of this tendency in a formal structure, a form of ecclesiastical organization that allowed a relatively high degree of congregational autonomy. The paradox of the theology of the church intensified the yearning for spirituality

and for corporateness, and because it did so, started the procession of ideas that passed through Independency to their clearest expression in Separatism—a strongly cellular corporate and participative kind of church polity.

Several of Cromwell's characteristic attitudes appear to derive from this complex of notions. His Churchmanship, for instance, was a flexible brand of Independency. It was both more and less than decentralized Calvinism: more, because he was more tolerant than his classical Independent brethren; and less than Independent because he refused to allow Parliament to frame a liturgy or even to articulate a list of damnable heresies. Moreover, his Establishment lacked any structure of disciplinary organisations, apart from the Commissions of Triers and Ejectors. His toleration was an integral part of his church system—for a Church of semi-autonomous consociations needed broad bosomed toleration as its necessary prerequisite and concomitant.

Cromwell's ability to associate with Fox or to parley with the Levellers on terms of ease and equity arose from his sensitive awareness of the communion of saints. And the fact that he did not feel a need to extend the franchise with his fellowship owed to that separation of the Church and the State in his mind, a separation implied by the Puritan view of the sanctity (and therefore the separateness) of the church in the world. What was true in the church did not have to apply in the state. Finally, and very tentatively, the yearning for corporateness engendered by Puritanism, found an outlet in Cromwell's curiously close relationship with his army officers. Though the officers' reputations leaned heavily upon his own, he shared or yielded political questions to groups among them until the close of his career.

Secondly, Puritanism made a paradox

of the nature of man. Man reflected the image of God and at the same time he was utterly depraved. The *imago dei* was twisted and distorted, because the leaven of original sin had permeated man's whole being and puffed up his every faculty with pride and rebellion. It is not suggested that Puritans and Puritans alone believed in the doctrine of original sin, simply that their view of man's corruption was especially harsh; and that as a result the contrast between the saved man and the sinner was particularly sharp. Cromwell's distinction between the "godly" and the "nation" is well known. So too is the primacy of his concern for the "good interests," and his scorn for constitutions, which he called, quoting Paul, "but dross and dung in comparison of Christ." What has perhaps been less apparent is that an extreme estimate of the Fall is a bulwark protecting the rights of private property; and further that Cromwell's theory of the purpose of State reflected his thoroughgoing pessimism about men in general. Government was a necessary evil, an expedient to preserve order, protect property, and forestall social anarchy. Even though he was Lord Protector of England, Scotland and Ireland, Cromwell continued to think of himself as a village constable appointed to keep the peace of the parish. His conception of the civil function of the government as limited to utilitarian ends is a view that foreshadows a stream of thought from Locke to John Stuart Mill.

Thirdly, accompanying this conception of government was a contrary tendency; a restless desire to improve the sinful world, even, as Milton said, to the Reformation of the Reformation itself. The urge had its origins in the paradox of Puritan metaphysics, in the constructions of the spheres of grace and nature. Though the word grace is a complex one in theological usage, it is here used loosely and simply to mean God's saving activity; and the word nature, to mean human nature rather than the physical universe. In Puritanism, grace and nature were incommensurate realms, and yet grace was involved with nature in a struggle, as it had to be in order to re-establish God's lost dominion over man. In other words, grace and nature were both radically separated and also joined with each other in a dialectical tension. Now this macrocosmic process operated on the individual in microcosm. Grace and nature were locked in a struggle for possession of the soul, and in the saved person grace predominated, though it could never fully triumph until after his death. An awareness of his place in this process impelled the saved man to join the battle, to enlist in the cosmic combat between grace and human sin. And the efforts were all the stronger because the Puritan knew he was on the Lord's side. Puritan metaphysics thus produced an activism that flooded into a variety of channels. In Cromwell it found persistent expressions in his desire to rationalize administrative inequities in the law, in the incidence of tithes, in the redistribution of the electorate and the qualified extension of the franchise — as well as his willingness to oversee the morals of the nation.

Fourthly, another paradox contributed to his activism. The Puritan was convinced of his salvation at the same time that he was steeling himself for a severe last judgment. Objectively and subjectively the knowledge of assurance was sure and steadfast, and objectively and subjectively he was equally certain of a searching final examination in the Court of Heaven. There, of course, the reprobates would attempt to defend themselves, while the elect would stand silent, humbled and contrite. This tension of expectations was unavoidable in a religion that stretched between the polarities of God's sovereignty and man's depravity. On the one hand the Puritan could be arrogant. "What shall we do with this bauble?" Cromwell asked of the mace, the symbol of Parliamentary authority; "Here, take it away!" On the other hand he could be self-effacing and self-deprecating. He rubbed shoulders with humble men without condescension. He wanted to be painted for posterity "warts and all," and considered himself "the chief of sinners." His arrogance and humility reflected the contradictions of a sure assurance and an impending judgement.

Fifthly Puritanism maintained the ancient Pauline paradox of Christian liberty, and liberty in this sense was less a freedom from than a freedom for. Voluntary obedience to the gospel would free men from the burden of the law and from the duress of punishment and death; active dedication could unloose in the believer a new power to act righteously, a power or freedom beyond the capacity of ordinary sinners. Cromwell's confused notion of liberty becomes much clearer in the light of this paradox. "I said: you were a free Parliament," he told his first Protectorate Parliament, "and truly so you are—whilst you own the Government and Authority which called you hither." Parliament, he was saying, should recognize the extraordinary chain of Divine Providences which had put him in the place of constituted authority; then, and only then, would members be able to rise above their carnal fetters. By obeying God's chosen instrument they would, in effect, be freeing themselves for the virtuous business of legislating the settlement of the nation. Thus the doctrine of

Christian liberty tossed a potential justification to tyranny, and under its malleable rubric Oliver was able to claim right and liberty for actions most arbitrary.

Sixthly, the moral law was both hidden and revealed. When the injunctions of Scripture were explicit and the circumstances plain, the path of action was clearly apparent, but when the written revelation was obscure or absent, conscience was king. R. S. Paul has recently argued that Cromwell laboured under a dual ethic, a double standard of justice, one human and one divine. This is perhaps misleading because it is too clear. It could be more accurate to think of Cromwell's ethic as at once threefold and onefold, like the Trinity. God spoke to men through revealed impressions—one—and through natural reason—two—, and also He drew human judgement to accord with His own intentions by confronting man with immediate and unavoidable circumstances. "God will lead us to what shall be His way," said Cromwell, and "surely what God would have us do, He does not desire we should step out of our way for it." The force of circumstance formed a bridge between the Divine and the human intelligence so Providence—or Justice or Necessity—was none other than the hand of God in historic events. Cromwell's answer to the moral dilemma of Puritanism was a common one, as old, indeed, as the Hebrew prophets. In fact, Cromwell justified all his actions by contingencies, and his threefold ethic, involving grace, nature, and the bridge between them built by the Holy Spirit, became one. This might be taken as self-deception—even idolatry—yet it was the mainspring of his greatness. The fusion of ethical levels, demanding that he read events as they ran, explains his hesitancies and his determinations. It was the foundation of his strength of character. Without this ethic Cromwell would not be the Cromwell one remembers for it made him larger than life-size; it gave him his personal impact; his compelling sense of moral conviction; and continual confirmation in the justice of his cause. Hence the tripartite yet single ethic may properly belong at the hub of his fame.

Finally, a word about his constitutional failure. Trevor-Roper has argued that Cromwell was politically maladroit; Hill that he could not manage the leap from a militarily to a civilly constituted order; S. R. Gardiner that the nation was repelled by the use of the military power. Cromwell himself, in conversation with the republican Ludlow, bemoaned the fact that the nation was too fragmented to be ruled constructively. "What is it that you would have?" he asked. ". . . That the nation might be governed by its own consent," returned Ludlow. ". . . But where shall we find that consent?" wailed Oliver. Another consideration could be added to the array of arguments: Cromwell failed because he would not relinquish his churchmanship. One of his reasons for destroying the Rump was that a group of its members was persecuting the saints in Wales. His party jettisoned the Parliament of Saints because the radicals threatened to undermine the Church Establishment. His two Protectorate Parliaments were wrecked by a combination of republican and Presbyterians who traded as their basis of mutual support a commonwealth in return for a Presbyterian Establishment.

Religion and toleration were the causes Cromwell had fought for. "God brought it to that issue at last, and gave it to us by way of a redundancy, and at last it proved to be that which was most dear to us." He could not relinquish his principles, and so long as he held them his constitutional edifices were bound to topple. As long as he believed them too, he could not avoid his dependence upon the army, for only there was an organized body of opinion in rough accord with his own. If his political career is regarded as a personal tragedy the fatal flaw was that the churchman remained a churchman. While the political nation was clamouring for settlement on other grounds, the Puritan remained a pilgrim for his faith to the very end. His failure, as well as his attempts at settlement, exhibits a consistency that was congruent with the deepest springs of his being—the paradoxical insights of Puritanism.

Like Hill and New, though very much earlier, SAMUEL RAWSON GARDINER (1829–1902) regarded Cromwell as an inconsistent person, and laid the inconsistency to his Englishness. Following an Oxford education, Gardiner became Professor of Modern History at King's College in the University of London. Over a period of forty years, he issued eighteen volumes of close political narrative which drew on a wealth of unused evidence that he unearthed himself. His story covered the early Stuart, Civil War, Commonwealth, and early Protectorate years. Gardiner's life and work were models of dedication, diligence, and patience. What his volumes lack in flamboyance, they make up in sympathetic impartiality and trustworthiness; they are standard references to this day. Breadth and mastery of material underlined Gardiner's succinct public lectures on Cromwell. Delivered toward the end of his career, the lectures embodied Gardiner's determination to see history in the round instead of in fragments. It is a longing born, perhaps, of the plethora of views on Cromwell.*

Samuel Rawson Gardiner

Cromwell's Place in History

What then, is Cromwell's place in history? If we regard the course of the two centuries which followed his death, it looks as if all that need be said might be summed up in a few words. His negative work lasted, his positive work vanished away. His constitutions perished with him, his Puritanism descended from the proud position to which he had raised it, his peace with the Dutch Republic was followed by two wars with the United Provinces, his alliance with the French monarchy only led to a succession of wars with France lasting into the nineteenth century. All that lasted was the support given by him to maritime enterprise, and in that he followed the tradition of the Governments preceding him.

Yet, after all, the further we are removed from the days in which Cromwell lived, the more loth are we to fix our eyes exclusively on that part of his work which was followed by immediate results. It may freely be admitted that his efforts to establish the national life upon a new basis came to nothing, without thinking any the worse of the man for making the attempt. It is beginning to

---

*From S. R. Gardiner, *Cromwell's Place in History* (London, 1897) pp. 112–116.

be realised that many, if not all the experiments of the Commonwealth were but premature anticipations of the legislation of the nineteenth century, and it is also beginning to be realised that, whatever may be our opinion of some of Cromwell's isolated actions, he stands forth as the typical Englishman of the modern world. That he will ever be more than this is not to be expected. Even if Scotchmen forget the memories of Dunbar and Worcester, it is certain that Drogheda and Wexford will not pass out of the minds of Irishmen. It is in England that his fame has grown up since the publication of Carlyle's monumental work, and it is as an Englishman that he must be judged.

What may be fairly demanded alike of Cromwell's admirers and of his critics is that they shall fix their eyes upon him as a whole. To one of them he is the champion of liberty and peaceful progress, to another the forcible crusher of free institutions, to a third the defender of oppressed peoples, to a fourth the asserter of his country's right to dominion. Every one of the interpreters has something on which to base his conclusions. All the incongruities of human nature are to be traced somewhere or other in Cromwell's career. What is more remarkable is that this union of apparently contradictory forces is precisely that which is to be found in the English people, and which has made England what she is at the present day.

Many of us think it strange that the conduct of our nation should often appear to foreign observers in colours so different from those in which we see ourselves. By those who stand aloof from us we are represented as grasping at wealth and territory, incapable of imaginative sympathy with subject races, and decking our misconduct with moral sentiments intended to impose on the world. From our own point of view, the extension of our rule is a benefit to the world, and subject races have gained far more than they have lost by submission to a just and beneficent administration, whilst our counsels have always, or almost always, been given with a view to free the oppressed and to put a bridle in the mouth of the oppressor.

That both these views have truth in them no serious student of the present and the past can reasonably deny. Whatever we may say, we are and have been a forceful nation, full of vigorous vitality, claiming empire as our due, often with scant consideration for the feelings and desire of other peoples. Whatever foreigners may say, we are prone, without afterthought, to place our strength at the service of morality and even to feel unhappy if we cannot convince ourselves that the progress of the human race is forwarded by our action. When we enter into possession, those who look on us from the outside dwell upon the irregularity of our conduct in forcing ourselves into possession; whilst we, on the contrary, dwell upon the justice and order maintained after we have once established ourselves.

With Cromwell's memory it has fared as with ourselves. Royalists painted him as a devil. Carlyle painted him as the masterful saint who suited his peculiar Valhalla. It is time for us to regard him as he really was, with all his physical and moral audacity, with all his tenderness and spiritual yearnings, in the world of action what Shakespeare was in the world of thought, the greatest because the most typical Englishman of all time. This, in the most enduring sense, is Cromwell's place in history. He stands there, not to be implicitly followed as a model, but to hold up a mirror to ourselves, wherin we may see alike our weakness and our strength.

Suggestions for Further Reading

W. C. Abbott, *A Bibliography of Oliver Cromwell* (Cambridge, Mass., 1929), is the standard reference of Cromwell studies. It lists over 3,500 items and is supplemented by an "Addenda to Bibliography" in volume four of Abbott's *The Writings and Speeches of Oliver Cromwell* (Cambridge, Mass., 1937–47). A stylish presentation of the changing patterns of interpretation on Cromwell is contained in the first chapter of M. P. Ashley, *The Greatness of Oliver Cromwell* (New York, 1958). D. H. Pennington contributed a lively article in "Oliver Cromwell and the Historians" to the Cromwell tercentenary issue of *History Today,* September, 1958, pp. 598–605; and Paul H. Hardacre has listed most of the writing that have appeared since the appearance of Abbott's bibliography until 1960 in "Writings on Oliver Cromwell Since 1929," *Journal of Modern History,* XXX, 111 (1961), 1–14.

Apart from the attacks on Cromwell cited within by Heath and Ludlow, William Prynne mounted a blistering attack on him in *The Machiavellian Cromwellist* (London, 1648). James Fletcher in *The Perfect Politician* (London, 1660), gives a slightly more moderate and more sarcastic Royalist view. Even the judicious Edward Hyde, Earl of Clarendon, *The History of the Rebellion and Civil Wars in England,* ed. W. D. Macray, six vol., (Oxford, 1958), was impressed by Oliver's wickedness as much as his craft.

The first serious historical apology was by a devout nonconformed minister, Isaac Kimber, *The Life of Oliver Cromwell* (London, 1724), soon to be followed by John Banks, *Political Life of Oliver Cromwell* (London, 1739). Meanwhile, Gregorio Leti had patronized him for Italian readers as a tyrant without vice who "refused a crown of gold to wear one of steel," in *Historia e memorie recondite sopra alla vita de Oliver Cromwell,* two vols, (Amsterdam, 1692).

In the eighteenth century, both Whig and Tory authors tended to rely on the unfavorable Royalist chronicles of the earlier period. David Hume, however, in his *History of England,* two vols., (Edinburgh, 1754) showed some perplexity when he came to assess Cromwell. The great advance in Cromwell scholarship in this period can be traced to the diligent antiquarians who gathered materials for the later use of Cromwell scholars. Mark Noble, *Memoirs of the Protectorate—House of Cromwell* (London, 1784) was one such mine of information.

In the French Revolution, many writers labored comparisons between Cromwell and Napoleon. Henry Hallam, who did so in his *The Constitutional History of England* (London, 1827), was attacked by Lord Macaulay for doing so in the *Edinburgh Review* (1828).

But the first extensive Whig view of Cromwell came from the pen of a Frenchman rather than an Englishman. François Guizot was an early liberal minister under Louis Phillipe. His *L'Historie de la Revolution d'Angleterre,* two vols., (Paris, 1826–27) treated Cromwell sympathetically in the light of his manifold difficulties. Like John Morley, whose view is contained within, Guizot knew from experience the limitations on and the ephemeral nature of political success. He nevertheless placed Cromwell in the pantheon of those who had forwarded liberty and progress. Another French author, whose view is expressed above, may never have written had he not decided that it was impossible to translate the volcanic and flamboyant style of Carlyle's *Letters and Speeches of Oliver Cromwell,* two vols., (London, 1845), into French. Thus we gained Merle D'Aubigné's *Le Protecteur* (Paris, 1848), previously translated as *The Protector; A Vindication* (New York 1846–47), which raised Cromwell above the common herd as a Protestant hero.

It remained for S. R. Gardiner and John Buchan to pull Cromwell down to earth again and for Sir Charles Firth to see solid merits in his achievements.

Views that are quite different from the Victorians and post-Victorians can be found in Edward Bernstein, *Cromwell and Communism*, trans. H. J. Stenning (London, 1930). Bernstein was a celebrated Marxist revisionist. Theodore Roosevelt, the equally celebrated American President, wrote a biography, *Oliver Cromwell* (New York, 1900), painting him as something of a seventeenth century Rough Rider.

Hitler's rise to power elicited a spate of new interpretations. Apart from Abbott, one can list Sir Ernest Barker, *Oliver Cromwell and the English People*, (London, 1937), who noted similarities between Hitler and Cromwell but also drew careful distinctions. Haunted by the rise of fascism, M. P. Ashley wrote *Oliver Cromwell: The Conservative Dictator*, but in a new biography, cited in the first paragraph of this bibliographical note, he displayed his humility and integrity and reviewed his opinion in 1958 in the light of new thoughts. Buchan, cited within, Veronica Wedgewood, *Oliver Cromwell* (London 1939), and Sir Winston Churchill in his *History of the English Speaking Peoples*, four vols., (New York 1956–58) offered balanced counters to the tendency to see Cromwell lurking in the shadows of that time.

The concern of scholars like Paul and New with the religious background or the interest of H. R. Trevor-Roper and Christopher Hill in social background underlines the fact that Cromwell cannot be isolated either from the factors leading to the upheaval of the Civil War, or from the contending parties which emerged as the war progressed. Most scholars, indeed, do not venture assessments of Cromwell until they have researched broadly and thoroughly the Tudor and Stuart periods. S. R. Gardiner's monumental works include ·

The History of England . . . 1603–1642, ten vols., (London, 1883–84); *History of the Great Civil War, 1647–49*, four vols., (London, 1889–91); and *History of the Commonwealth and Protectorate, 1649–1656*, four vols., (London, 1903). Sir Charles Firth completed Gardiner's labors with studies of Scotland during the civil wars and with *The Last Years of the Protectorate*, two vols., (London, 1909). With Godfrey Davies, Firth wrote *The Regimental History of Cromwell's Army*, two vols., (Oxford, 1937). Godfrey Davies wrote the volume in the Oxford series on *The Early Stuarts*, (Oxford, 1937) and compiled an indispensable general bibliography of the Stuart period. For a fresh and limpid narrative history of the coming, waging, and ending of the war, C. V. Wedgewood has written *The King's Peace* (London, 1955), *The King's Wars* (London, 1958), and *Trial of Charles First* (London, 1964). A sound and more compressed study is Ivan Roots' *The Great Rebellion, 1642–1660* (London, 1966), while Christopher Hill has written a splendid interpretive text, *Century of Revolution, 1603–1714* (Edinburgh, 1961). Gerald Aylmer offers a brief introduction to the period in *The Struggle for the Constitution*, 1603–1689 (London, 1963).

A slight sampling of the controversy on the gentry and of the shifts in power and influence of various social classes before the war, which many believe to be crucial to the coming of the war and Cromwell's part in it, would include R. H. Tawney, "The Rise of the Gentry, 1540–1640," *Economic History Review*, Supplement No. 1, 1952; J. H. Hexter, "Storm over the Gentry," *Encounter*, May, 1958; Pevery Zagorin, "The Social Interpretation of the English Revolution," *Journal of Economic History*, XIX (1959), 376–401; and Lawrence Stone, *The Crisis of the Aristocracy, 1558–1641* (Oxford, 1965).

Varying assessments of the importance of religion in the coming of the war may be found in R. H. Tawney, *Religion and the Rise of Capitalism* (London 1926), who found psychic similarities between Puritanism and the new thrusting spirit of capitalism; Christopher Hill, *The Economic Problems of the Church*

(Oxford, 1956), who attached the growing weakness of the church to its financial plight and implied that attempts to recoup wealth aroused fears that private property would be endangered. Paul S. Seaver, however, in *The Puritan Lectureships* (Stanford, 1970), has shown that Puritan energy and drive overcame financial obstacles within the apparatus of the church to set up preaching propaganda posts in London especially. John F. H. New, *Anglican and Puritan . . . 1558-1640* (Stanford and London, 1964) has argued that the issues between the sides were of a fairly profound philosophical and theological nature. William Haller, *Liberty and Reformation in the Puritan Reformation* (New York, 1955) and Michael Walzer, *Revolt of the Saints* (Cambridge, Mass., 1965) emphasize the role of ideology in the coming and progress of the revolution.

For the development of parties in the early years of the Long Parliament, J. H. Hexter, *The Reign of King Pym* (Cambridge, Mass., 1941) is indispensable. George Yule, *The Independents in the English Civil War* (Cambridge, 1958) studied the rather loose party which Cromwell aligned himself with in the war period. His findings have been challenged in detail and successfully defended in general in the periodical literature. The first detailed studies of members of the Long Parliament were undertaken by Mary Friar Keeler, *The Long Parliament, 1640-41* (Philadelphia, 1954) and D. Brunton and D. H. Pennington, *Members of the Long Parliament* (London, 1954). The close affinity between religious and political postures suggested in their works is corroborated in an article by Lotte Glow, "Political Affiliation in the House of Commons after Pym's Death," *Institute of Historical Research Bulletin*, XXXVIII (May, 1965) 48-70.

Although Seaver has recently shown just how far London was studded with Puritan lectureships, the long accepted claim that London was from the first a Parliamentary stronghold was upset up Valerie Pearl, *London and the Outbreak of the Puritan Revolution* (London, 1961). The larger financiers and merchants, it appears, were timid; and London became strongly Parliamentary only

when their moderating influence was swept away by men from lower echelons, with more virile enthusiasms and fears. The lower house of Parliament, and Cromwell, had to ally with lower social classes in order to swell the strength of their cause. From that enlistment, reluctant in one case and eager in the other, grew a political articulation of petit-bourgeois aims known as the Leveller movement. Joseph Frank, *The Levellers* (Cambridge, Mass., 1958) and H. N. Brailsford, *The Levellers and the English Revolution* (Stanford, 1961) are two good studies. C. B. MacPherson has shown that Levellers were not the democrats they have been thought to be in *The Political Theory of Possessive Industrialism* (Oxford, 1962). A. S. P. Woodhouse edited the debates in the Army Council between officers and Leveller representatives of the rank and file in *Puritanism and Liberty* (London, 1938), and he added both supporting documents and a profound introduction. William Haller and Godfrey Davies edited some *Leveller Tracts, 1647-53* (New York, 1966), and D. M. Wolfe has edited *Levellers' Manifestoes of the Puritan Revolution* (New York, 1966).

A good beginning for the political thought of the period in general is J. W. Allen, *English Political Thought, 1603-1660* (London, 1938). Prevery Zagorin, *A History of Political Thought in the English Revolution* (London, 1956) touches on radicalism; and Vera S. Finch, *The Classical Republicans* (Evanston, 1965) deals with the ideas of the doctrinaire Commonwealthmen who gave Cromwell so much trouble in his Protectorate Parliaments.

C. H. Firth and R. S. Rait put all students in their debt by editing *The Acts and Ordinances of the Interregnum*, three vols., (London, 1911). Old, but still valuable studies are Edward Jenks, *The Constitutional Experiments of the Commonwealth* (Cambridge, Mass., 1890) and F. A. Inderwick, *The Interregnum* (London, 1891). A more recent study of the ideas underlying the experiments of the Interregnum is J. W. Gough, *Fundamental Law in English Constitutional History*, (Oxford, 1955). David Masson, *Life of Milton*, seven vols., (Cambridge, 1859-1894), another book covering the Interregnum period, is much broader than the title suggests.

Biographies abound about the many friends and foes Cromwell made in his lifetime and the many acquaintances with whom he associated from time to time including army officers, administrators, political leaders, writers, and men of a variety of religious hues. There are numerous special studies of Cromwell's associates. One general study is A. H. Woolrych, *Battles of the English Civil War* (New York, 1951). P. H. Hardacre discussed *The Royalists during the Puritan Revolution* (The Hague, 1956) and David Underdown the *Royalist Conspiracy in England, 1649–1660* (New Haven, 1960).

An older reliable history of the institutional religious changes in the period is W. A. Shaw, *A History of the English Church during the Civil War and under the Commonwealth 1640–1660,* two vols., (London, 1900). G. F. Nuttall had added sympathetic insight into religious thought with *The Holy Spirit in Puritan Faith and Experience* (Oxford, 1946) and *Visible Saints: The Congregational Way* (Oxford, 1957). Christopher Hill once again explores the mundane purposes served by Puritanism in *Society and Puritanism in Pre-Revolutionary England* (London 1966). W. K. Jordan, *The Development of Religious Toleration in England,* four vols., (Cambridge, Mass., 1932–1940) devotes much of volume three to this period. Leo Solt offers a less hopeful assessment of Puritan ideology in *Saints in Arms* (Stanford, 1959).

On Cromwellian policy beyond Britain one must look to volume one of *The Cambridge History of the British Empire* (Cambridge, 1929), which covers the Interregnum. Charles Wilson, *Profit and Power: A Study of England and the Dutch Wars* (London, 1957) is an important study. R. W. K. Hinton, *The Eastland Trade and the Commonwealth in the Seventeenth Century* (Cambridge, 1959) covers a neglected topic. A good general survey of economic and industrial development has been offered by Christopher Hill, *Reformation to Industrial Revolution,* (London, 1967). M. P. Ashley, *Financial and Commercial Policy under the Cromwellian Protectorate* (Oxford, 1936) is a most useful general study on a more limited period. On the social side, there is Margaret James, *Social Problems and Policy during the Puritan Revolution* (London, 1930). These older works can be and need to be supplemented by a host of articles on special problems ranging from agrarian legislation and poor relief to the sale of Royalist lands and projects for law reform in the period.

Although the burden of obtaining a thorough grounding in the period rests heavily on the student of Cromwell, it may be true that the most prolonged steeping in the evidence will still not enable him to recapture the precise flavor of the time and of the man who dominated it. In an old biography of *Cromwell,* Eucardio Momigliano began, "It is the fatal destiny of a man who issues from a revolution, and has drawn upon himself unlimited hatred and boundless admiration to have no impartial biographers." Perhaps so, yet all might agree to transfer to Cromwell Gibbon's comment on Belisarius: while his errors and failings were those of his country and party, his strength and virtues were his own.